CW00323807

Los Angeles

United States

EVERYMAN
CITY GUIDES

EVERYMAN CITY GUIDES
Copyright © 2001 Everyman
Publishers Ltd, London

ISBN 1-84159-027-4

First published April 2001

Originally published in France
by Nouveaux Loisirs, a
subsidiary of Gallimard, Paris
2000, and in Italy by Touring
Editore, Srl., Milano 2000.
Copyright © 2000
Nouveaux Loisirs,
Touring Editore, Srl.

SERIES EDITORS: Anne-Josyane
Magniant & Marisa Bassi
LOS ANGELES EDITION:
Sophie Lenormand *assisted by*
Andrew Bender in Los Angeles
LAYOUT: Olivier Lauga
GRAPHICS: Yann Le Duc *assisted
by* Isabelle Dubois-Dumée
MAPS: Édigraphie
STREET MAPS: Touring Club Italiano
PRODUCTION: Catherine
Bourrabier

Translated by Susan Liddington
Edited and typeset by First Edition
Translations Ltd, Cambridge, UK

Printed in Italy by
Editoriale Lloyd

*Note from the publisher:
To keep the price of this guide as
low as possible we decided on a
common edition for the UK and
US which has meant American
spelling.*

Authors
LOS ANGELES

Getting there:
Sophie Lenormand (1)
Born with a suitcase in her hand, Sophie has
been on the road since her earliest years. Her
travels throughout the world, in particular to
the United States, mean that she has the right
knowledge to get you there safe and sound.

Where to stay: Andrew Bender (2)
Totally enamored of his adopted city, Andy
Bender shares this enthusiasm through his
food column in the *Westside Weekly* section
of the *L.A. Times*. Author of numerous
reports for *Travel & Leisure* magazines, he
regularly writes articles on hotels for
Fortune, In Style and *Philadelphia Inquirer*.

Where to eat: Karen Berk (3)
Co-editor of Zagat *Los Angeles Restaurants*
and *Marketplaces* since 1986, Karen is also
author of the *California Cooking* and *Los
Angeles Food Guide* cook books. When she
isn't trying out L.A.'s restaurants, this vice-
president of the *Dames d'Escoffier* (a
worldwide society of high-achieving women
in the fields of food, fine beverage and
hospitality) is teaching the culinary arts in
her own establishment, The Seasonal Table
Cooking School.

After dark: Scott Arundale and Regan Kibbee (4)
Scott and Regan have been club promoters
in Los Angeles for more than ten years, and
share a passion for world music. At the
same time, Scott, a former DJ, produces
music films and videos, while Regan supplies
details on the Internet of where to go for
nights out in the city.

What to see and Further afield: Valerie Summers (5)
Publisher and editor of the *Southern California
Guide* for almost twenty years, Valerie runs
the *S.C.G.* and *Travellady* Internet sites. Born in
L.A. and a worldwide traveler, she has
contributed to the New Orleans *Clarion
Ledger*, to the Indiana magazine *Journeys* and
to the businessman's guide *Bradman's*.

Where to shop:
Andrea Schulte-Peevers (6)
The sun, the sea and her future husband
brought A. Schulte-Peevers to Los Angeles in
1987. Co-author of guides to Los Angeles and
California, she contributes to *Conde Nast
Traveller* magazine and the *L.A. Business Journal,
San Diego Tribune* and *Denver Post* newspapers.

Symbols

- ☎ telephone
- ➠ fax
- ● price or price range
- 🕒 opening hours
- 🗀 credit cards accepted
- 🗗 credit cards not accepted
- 🆅 toll-free number
- @ e-mail/website address
- ★ tips and recommendations

Access

- Ⓜ subway stations
- 🚌 bus (or tram)
- Ⓟ private parking
- 🅿️ parking attendant
- ♿ no facilities for the disabled
- 🚆 train
- 🚗 car
- ⛴ boat

Hotels

- ☎ telephone in room
- 🖷 fax in room on request
- 🍾 minibar
- 📺 television in room
- 🅰️ air-conditioned rooms
- 🕐 24-hour room service
- caretaker
- 👶 babysitting
- 🏢 meeting room(s)
- 🐾 no pets
- 🍳 breakfast
- ☕ open for tea/coffee
- 🍴 restaurant
- 🎵 live music
- 💿 disco
- 🌳 garden, patio or terrace
- 🏋️ gym, fitness club
- 🏊 swimming pool, sauna

Restaurants

- 🥗 vegetarian food
- 🏔️ view
- 👔 formal dress required
- 🚬 smoking area
- 🍸 bar

Museums and galleries

- 🏛️ on-site store(s)
- 🧭 guided tours
- ☕ café

Stores

- 🏬 branches, outlets

The Insider's Guide is made up of **8 sections**, each indicated by a different color.

Things you need to know (mauve)
Where to stay (blue)
Where to eat (red)
After dark (pink)
What to see (green)
Further afield (orange)
Where to shop (yellow)
Finding your way (purple)

In the area
Where to stay: ➤ 34
After dark: ➤ 8
What to see: ➤ 86 ➤ 106 ➤ 110
Where to shop: ➤ 126

Where to

King's Fish House / King Crab Lou
100 W. Broadway, Long Beach, CA 90802 ☎ 562
(Pine Ave) Ⓟ **Seafood** ●●● 🕒 Sun.–Thu. 11.15am–
10pm; Fri., Sat. 11.15am–11pm...

Actually two restaurants under one roof, the Fish House
and casual dining, with a clubby sensibility while the King Crab
tablecloth dining, with a clubby sensibility... Long Beach
streets, it has formal and expensive than its Downtown sib
Grill. It uses formal and expensive than its Downtown sib
includes several spicy New Orleans-style shrimp dishes...

(Pine Ave) Ⓟ **Seafood** ●●●
10pm; Fri., Sat. 11.15am–11

Practical information is given for each particular establishment: opening times, prices, ways of paying, different services available.

Frenchy's Bistro (76)
(between Termino and Ximeno Ave) ☎ French ●●● 🕒 Tue.–
2.30pm, 5.30–9.30pm; Fri. 11.30am–2.30pm, 5.30–10.30 Sat. S...
This friendly sleeper is one of Long Beach's best-kept sec
warm, neighborhood feel and makes every customer feel welcome. Th
owners and staff in this city full of tempting-sounding dishes. T
inspire and name is filled with such... provi
chops on cob polenta, and a balsamic-laced currant reduc
pistachio crusted salmon on cold brandade with tomato b

Belmont Brewing (77)
Belmont Pier, 25 39th Place, Long Beach, CA 90803 ☎
(Ocean Blvd) Ⓟ **Eclectic American** ●● 🕒 Mon.–Fri
Sat. 10pm; Sun 9pm... amous Pier h
This laid-back brewpub at the foot of the... amous Pier h
boardwalk. Southern California quality seafood and a great place to
one of the best brewpubs... to eat; there's everything tra
sandwiches, pizza and baby back ribs with garlic mashe
with cilantro pasta...

Not Forgetting
☎ **Sir Jormston's (78)** 1126 Queen's Highw
CA 90802 ☎ 562/435-3511... The menu is somewhat dow
conference food is more... on be most at... popular dist
attraction. ☎ **Shenandoah Café (79)** 4722 E. Second St
CA 90803 ☎ 562/434-3469... This charming country restaur

How to use this guide

In the area
- Where to stay: ➡ 34
- After dark: ➡ 8
- What to see: ➡ 86 ➡ 106 ➡
- Where to shop: ➡ 126

The section **"In the area"** refers you (➡ 00) to other establishments that are covered in a different section of the guide but found in the same area of the city.

Long Beach   F C3-4 - D3-4

The small map shows all the establishments mentioned and others described elsewhere but found "in the area", by the color of the section.

The name of the district is given above the map. A grid reference (**A** B-C 2) enables you to find it in the section on Maps at the end of the book.

Not forgetting

■ **Sir Winston's (78)** Queen Mary CA 90802 ☎ 562/435-3511 ●●●● The

The section "Not forgetting" lists other useful addresses in the same area.

⭐ **"Bargain!"**
This star marks good value hotels and restaurants.

The opening page to each section contains an index ordered alphabetically (Getting there), by subject or by district (After dark) as well as useful addresses and advice.

The section "Things you need to know" covers information on getting to London and day-to-day life in the city.

Theme pages introduce a selection of establishments on a given topic.

The "Maps" section of this guide contains 9 street plans of London followed by a detailed index.

Time difference
The time difference between the UK and the west coast of the US is 8 hours, between the east and west coasts of the US 5 hours.

Getting ther

Health insurance
The cost of treatment is high and hospitals will not accept patients who do not have health insurance. Travelers from outside the US should take out insurance before leaving home. This is offered by travel agencies, or may be among the services offered by your credit card.

Toll free numbers
Calls to these numbers, which start with 800 or 888, are free within the US. It is possible to call them from some other countries, including the UK, where they are charged at the standard international rate.

Electrical current
The US electrical system operate at 110 Volts and 60 Hz, requiring pin plugs with flat pins. You will ne an adaptor and a transformer to equipment from outside the US.

Things you
42
need to know

Formalities

UK citizens do not require a visa for stays of less than ninety days, but your passport must be valid six months after the date of return. It is illegal to bring in any plants or perishable produce.

Embassies and consulates

British Consulate: Suite 400, 11766 Wilshire Blvd, Los Angeles, CA 90025-6538 ☎ 310/477 3322

Australian Embassy: 611 North Larchmont Blvd, Los Angeles, CA 90004-9998 ☎ 213/469 4300

Canadian Embassy: 300 South Grand Ave, 10th Floor, Los Angeles, CA 90071 ☎ 213/687 7432

Public holidays

On these days, Angelinos are out of town and most institutions and public services are closed. Museums and restaurants strictly observe closing days on Thanksgiving, Christmas and New Year.

New Year's Day January 1
Martin Luther King Jr.'s Day Third Monday in January
President's Day Third Monday in February
Easter Monday
Memorial Day Last Monday in May
Independence Day July 4 (national holiday)
Labor Day First Monday in September
Columbus Day Second Monday in October
Veterans Day November 11 (Armistice)
Thanksgiving Day Fourth Thursday in November
Christmas December 25

INDEX

Basic facts

International flights come into LAX, Los Angeles' international airport, located by the sea south of Santa Monica. Domestic flights use LAX, Burbank and Long Beach airports. Burbank and Long Beach are about fourteen miles and twenty-two miles respectively from Downtown L.A.

Getting there

Airports

LAX (1)
L.A. International Airport
Information
☎ 310/646-5252
Most national and international flights land at LAX, the fourth largest airport in the world in terms of traffic. It has nine terminals including TBIT (Tom Bradley International Terminal). Arrivals are on the lower level and departures on the upper level.
Theme building
At the very top of this theme building you will find The Encounter, the restaurant for members of the jet set. Ideal for that last drink before take-off.

The Encounter
☎ 310/215-5151
◷ Sun.–Wed. 11am–midnight; Thu.–Sat. 11am–1.30am
Tourist information
Travelers Aid
You will find booths on the arrivals level of each terminal.
☎ 310/646-2270
◷ daily 6am–9pm
Quick Aid
Touchscreens give you all types of information.
Courtesy telephones
These telephones enable you to book hotel rooms, rent a car, etc.
Lost & Found
☎ 310/417-0440
Police
☎ 310/646-7911
Customs
☎ 310/215-2414

LAX Shuttles
These free shuttles, white with green and blue stripes, will transfer you to another terminal or to the parking lot. The 'A' Shuttle makes a circular tour of the airport.
◷ 24-hour service

Burbank (2)
Information
☎ 818/840-8847
Located about fourteen miles to the northwest of Downtown L.A., this airport represents a good alternative if you are taking a domestic flight. There is a regular free shuttle service between Downtown and Burbank.

Long Beach Airport (3)
Information
☎ 562/570-2600
A small domestic airport, located about six miles from the center of Long Beach.

Airport connections

Courtesy trams
The major hotels charter their own free shuttles or limos. Just signal them to stop.
Van Stop
These minibuses, which will charge you less than the taxi fare, operate 24 hours a day and will take you to any address. The choice of company depends on destination. Inquire at the ground transportation

booth located next to the luggage carousels.
● *$22 approx.*
Prime Shuttle
☎ *800/262-7433*
Super Shuttle
☎ *310/782-6600*
Coast Shuttle
☎ *310/417-3988*
Bus
The LAX 'C' Shuttle will take you to the LAX Transit Center where you can take an MTA bus (➜ 11). For Downtown take the no. 439, and for West Hollywood and Beverly Hills the no. 220. Information at the ground transportation booths or by telephone at: ☎ *213/626-4455*
Metro Rail
The LAX 'G' Shuttle sets you down at the Green Line station Aviation on Vicksburg Ave and 96th St. See map ➜ 11.

● *$1.35 approx*
Taxi
Expensive, considering the distances covered. A dispatcher will give you a leaflet listing the set rates.
● *$28 approx. for Downtown; $32 for Hollywood; $95 for Disneyland*

Car rental
Take the company's free shuttle that passes in front of all terminals. To leave the airport or to find your way back, ask for a map from the rental company.
● *$25-45 approx. per day; $120-200 a week plus 8.25% tax; $9-11 per day for LDW (loss-damage-waiver) insurance; $20 approx. per day for LSI- (liability supplement insurance)*
Alamo
☎ *800/327-9633*

Avis
☎ *800/831-2847*
Budget
☎ *800/527-0700*
Entreprise
☎ *800/736-8222*
Hertz
☎ *800/654-3131*
National
☎ *800/227-7968*
Thrifty
☎ *800/367-2277*

Train
Take the Coast Starlight that runs along the west coast from Seattle, the Sunset Limited that crosses the Southern States from Florida, or even the Southeast Chief which leaves from the east coast passing through Chicago. All trains arrive at *Union Station (4) 800 N. Alameda St.* ☎ *213/683-6979*
Amtrak
To find out timetables and fares:
☎ *800/872-7245*
www.amtrack.com

Long-distance bus
Los Angeles is served by Greyhound buses, departing from all major American cities. Vehicles are comfortable and air-conditioned and rates are attractive, although some air fares may be cheaper.
Greyhound
☎ *800/231-2222*
Depending on your destination, you have the choice of four bus stations:
Downtown (5)
Terminus principal 1716 E. 7th Street (Alameda St.)
☎ *213/629-8421*
Hollywood (6)
1409 N. Vine St.
☎ *323/466-9384*
Santa Monica (7)
4th St. (between Colorado Blvd and Broadway)
Long Beach (8)
464 W. 3rd St.
☎ *562/432-7780*

Basic facts

You don't walk in Los Angeles, you drive. Here, where the car rules, the network of freeways extends over 1,000 miles, facilitating direct access by road to every city. Buses run the length and breadth of the county, and are a cheap way to visit the various districts of L.A.

Getting there

By car

Unless you have a lot of time to spare, or are on a very limited budget, the car is the only practical means of getting around. There are, however, certain very Californian rules that need to be respected and, when possible, avoid peak hours (7–10am and 3–7pm).

Thomas Guide
This 'bible' is the inseparable companion of people living in Los Angeles. It is an indexed road map of the city, and is sold in bookstores.

Radio traffic information
To check on the state of roads around the clock.

*KNX 1070 AM
KFWB 980 AM*

Freeways
Don't be put off! L.A. freeways are possibly the fastest and easiest-to-use roads in the world. Nevertheless, you will find it useful to memorize their names and numbers. The general rule is that even numbers go from east to west, and odd numbers from north to south. (Numbers and names of the freeways ➡ 146)

Highway code
As well as the usual international driving rules (wearing of seatbelts, etc.), there are some distinctive Californian regulations to be aware of.

Speed
As a general rule, speed is limited in urban areas to 35mph, and on the freeways to 65mph. Watch out! You can be warned for excessively slow driving as well as for speeding. Also be aware that helicopters are monitoring you.

Red lights
Unless otherwise indicated you can turn right at a red light, but you must still give way to cars and pedestrians.

Diamond lanes
Sometimes on the freeways, the lane on the extreme left of the roadway is separated from the others by a double yellow line. This is a diamond lane, exclusively for use by car pools, or vehicles carrying more than two people. Do a head count unless you want to pay a fine of over $300!

Stop All Way
Crossroads frequently have four stop signs. Priority is given to the first car that arrives. If two or more cars arrive at the same time, priority reverts to the one on the right.

Parking
Parking in the road in some districts is a real feat, and can cost a small fortune
● 25 ¢ approx./ 15min

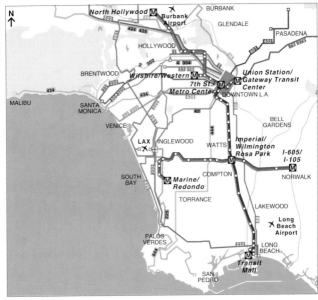

Fines
The police do not stop at just giving you a warning: a ticket can cost you a minimum of $38 for exceeding the time limit or parking illegally.

Road signs and markings
Parking in some residential areas is prohibited in the evenings, at peak times (on main roads) or when roads are being cleaned, etc. Pay particular attention to the colored lines on the sidewalk: red: prohibited; yellow: delivery; white: picking up or setting down; green: 20 mins. max.; blue: disabled. For greater peace of mind, use parking spaces that give rates by the hour or by the day. Those a little out of town offer more attractive rates.

By motorbike
You can easily fulfill your dream of making out you're an 'Easy Rider', racing down that mythical Route 66 to the Pacific Ocean at Santa Monica. What's more, the climate is idyllic.
● *$75-150 per day*
Rent a Custom Harley-Davidson
4161 Lincoln Blvd, Marina del Rey
☎ *310/578-0112*
Eaglerider
20917 Western Ave, Torrence
☎ *310/320-3456*

On foot
Angelinos will try to dissuade you, but don't be put off as some districts are well worth exploring on foot. But don't forget to observe the rules for pedestrians. Jaywalking is punishable by a heavy fine.

Buses
More than 208 bus routes crisscross the city. This vast network is managed by several companies.

Metropolitan Transit Authority (MTA)
Several information bureaus (all closed at the weekend) including:
ARCO Plaza, floor C, 515 Flower St.
☎ *800/266-6883*
🕐 *Mon.–Fri. 7.30am–3.30pm*
Some buses, such as the no. 2 that runs along Sunset Boulevard or no. 434 to Malibu, will give you the chance to see L.A. at low cost.
🕐 *5–2am; every 15 mins*
● *$1.35; transfer 25¢; freeway express $1.85-3.85*

DASH
The Downtown Area Short Hop covers Down-town L.A. from Chinatown to Exposition Park.
☎ *213 808-2273*

🕐 *Daily 6.30am–6.30pm; every 6–15 mins* ● *25 ¢*

Big Blue Bus
This service from the town of Santa Monica covers the whole of L.A.'s Westside. The no. 14 will take you to the Getty Center and the no. 10 to Downtown L.A.
☎ *310/253-6500*
🕐 *5.30am–midnight daily (Sun. from 6.30am)*
● *50 ¢; freeway express $1.25*

Metro Rail
The network has three lines:
Blue line
Downtown – Long Beach
Red line
Downtown – Universal City
Green line
Redondo Beach – Norwalk (connection with the Blue line at Imperial/Wilmington)
● *$1.35*
🕐 *5am–11pm; every 15 mins*

Accidents
In an emergency call 911.

Basic facts

Angelinos have a reputation for their fabulous shows and parties, but in reality they go to bed early. However, they also get up early: the day begins at 6am (with a jog) and rarely ends later than 10pm, or 2am for the real party-goers. Pick up the rhythm and, helped by the climate, you'll have no problem.

Getting by

Tourist information

Los Angeles Convention and Visitors Bureau
Downtown L.A.
685 S. Figueroa St.
☎ 213/689-8822
🕐 Mon.–Fri.
8am–5pm; Sat.
8.30am–5pm
Hollywood
Janes House, 6541
Hollywood Blvd
☎ 213/689-8822
🕐 Mon.–Sat.
9am–5pm
Some towns have their own tourist offices.
Beverly Hills
239 S. Beverly Dr.
☎ 310/271-8174
🕐 Mon.–Fri.
8.30am–5pm
Long Beach
1 World Trade
Center, Suite 300
☎ 562/436-3645
Pasadena
171 S. Los Robles
Avenue

☎ 626/795-9311
Santa Monica (1)
520 Broadway,
Suite 250
☎ 310/319-6263
🕐 Mon.–Fri.
9am–5pm
1400 Ocean Blvd,
☎ 310/393-7593
🕐 daily 9am–6pm

Money

Checks are rarely used.
Coins/notes (2)
The currency unit is the dollar ($) divided into 100 cents (¢). Avoid banknotes larger than $50 as these may not be accepted. Coins are called penny (1¢), nickel (5¢), dime (10¢) and quarter (25¢). Always have a number of quarters with you for using in parking meters and vending

machines and on public transport.
Exchange
$ 1 = 60–70p
Thomas Cook
To find the nearest office, contact:
☎ 800/287-7362
Banks
The largest in L.A. are Bank of America, First Federal and Union Bank.
🕐 Mon.–Thu.
10am–5pm; Fri.
10am–6pm;
Sat.10am–1pm
Cashpoints
Apart from banks, an increasing number of businesses (from gas stations to grocers) have their own cashpoints.
Credit cards
In addition to their regular use for purchases, they are essential for making

reservations by telephone and for the deposit when renting a car.
Taxes
Not included in the marked price. Add 8.25% for most goods and services. Hotel taxes ➡ 14.
Tips
Tips are never included in the bill and should be added on, unless the service was very bad; bars and restaurants between 15% and 20%; taxis 10-15%.

The media

Papers (3)
Available in most hotels, in kiosks or in vending machines on street corners.
Dailies (4)
Los Angeles Times;
Daily News; Orange
County Register;

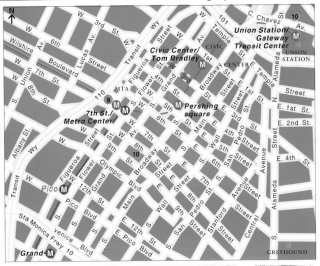

Long Beach Press Telegram; Pasadena Star News

Magazines (5)

L.A. Magazine; zeitgeist Specializing in the world of show biz: *Variety; Hollywood Reporter*

Free (6)

Excellent sources for show details. *L.A. Weekly; New Times; Showtime; The Argonaut*

International press

Universal News Agency 1655 N. Las Palmas, Hollywood ☎ 213/467-3850 🕒 10am–midnight

Farmer's Market 6333 W. Third Ave, Los Angeles 🕒 8am–7pm

Radios

There are over 100 FM radio stations in Los Angeles.

88.1 KLON (jazz); 101.1 KRTH (rock); 105.1 KKGO (classical music); 106.7 KROQ (alternative rock)

Telephone (7)

Information

☎ 411 ☎ 0 (operator)

How to dial

For all numbers in the same call area, simply dial the seven digits of the phone number. Outside this area, dial 1 followed by the code, then the number.

L.A. dialing codes 213 Downtown; 323 Hollywood; 310 Beverly Hills, West L.A., Santa Monica, South Bay; 626 Pasadena; 818 San Fernando; 562 Long Beach

International Dial code 011 followed by the country code: Australia 61; Ireland 353; New Zealand 64; United Kingdom 44

Phone cards

In hotels, an extra 50¢ to $1.50 may be added to the price of calls, even when local! Use phone cards instead. These are available from tourist offices.

● $10, 20 or 30

Collect calls ☎ 1-800/473-7262

Mail (8)

Use the boxes with blue lettering marked 'US Mail'.

● $1 for Europe

Downtown L.A. 900 N. Alameda Ave ☎ 213/617-4641 🕒 Mon.–Fri. 8am–5pm; Sat. 9am–noon

Embassies & consulates

🕒 Mon.–Fri. 9am–noon

Australian Embassy 611 North Larchmont Blvd, Los Angeles, CA 90004-9998 ☎ 213/469 4300

British Consulate Suite 400, 11766 Wilshire Blvd, Los Angeles, CA 90025-6538 ☎ 310/477 3322

Canadian Embassy 300 South Grand Ave, 10th Floor, Los Angeles, CA 90071 ☎ 213/687 7432

Emergencies

Police, fire service, ambulance, etc. ☎ 911 (free)

Police LAPD ☎ 213/485-3294

Cutting the cost

Many hotels offer weekend packages, corporate rates aimed at companies but also available to individuals and reductions for retired people or members of automobile clubs, as well as rates for a long stay. Don't be afraid to ask for a reduction, negotiate in advance and get it confirmed in writing.

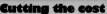

Where to stay

Famous hotel bars

Trader Vic's ➡ 70 (Beverly Hilton Hotel)
Bar Marmont ➡ 72 (Chateau Marmont)
The Sky Bar ➡ 72 (Mondrian Hotel)
Toppers (Radisson Huntley Hotel)
Gallery Bar (Regal Biltmore Hotel)
Top of the Five (Westin Bonaventure Hotel)

Tips

Usually:
Chambermaid $1 per day
Bellboy $1 per item of luggage
Car attendant $1 to $2
Concierge $5

Prices For a standard double room, the prices given do not include tax. Add the government tax, plus 14% tourist tax. Rates vary according to season and availability: they can double in convention periods and in the high season (Feb.–Oct.).

68
Hotels

Hotel chains

They can be found in the most strategic locations in Los Angeles.

Economy ($50-90)
Day Inn ☎ 800/325-2525
Econo Lodge ☎ 800/446-6900
Motel 6 ☎ 800/466-8356
Super 8 Motel ☎ 800/800-8000
Travel Lodge ☎ 800/255-3050
Vagabond Inn ☎ 800/522-1555

Mid-range ($90-170)
Best Western ☎ 800/528-1234
Comfort Inn ☎ 800/228-5150
Howard Johnson ☎ 800/654-2000
Quality Inn ☎ 800/228-5151
Radisson ☎ 800/333-3333
Ramada Inn ☎ 800/272-6232

INDEX BY PRICE

In the area
- ▪️ **Where to eat:** ➡ 38 ➡ 40
- ▪️ **After dark:** ➡ 74
- ▪️ **What to see:** ➡86 ➡ 88 ➡ 90
- ▪️ **Where to shop:** ➡ 128

➡ Where to stay

Westin Bonaventure Hotel & Suites (1)
404 S. Figueroa Street, Los Angeles, CA 90071 ☎ 213/624-1000

(between 4th and 5th Sts) Ⓜ *7th St., Pershing Square* 🅿️ 🈁 *1,354 rooms (176 suites)* ●●● ▭ ⏰ ▣ 🈂️ 🏧 🛗 Ⅲ 🍴 🍸 *Lobby Court* 🖥️ *Market* 🏪 🎾 ♨️ ✚ ≋ ✂️ ▦ ★ ☘️ 📺 800/937-8461 @ abon@westin.com

Five glass cylindrical towers of 35 stories each, this vast hotel built in the mid-1970s covers an entire city block, with innumerable shopping and dining options.

Wyndham Checkers Hotel (2)
535 S. Grand Avenue, Los Angeles, CA 90071 ☎ 213/624-0000

(6th St.) Ⓜ *7th St., Pershing Square* 🅿️ 🈁 *188 rooms (2 suites)* ●●● ▭ ⏰ ▣ 🈂️ 🏧 *Checkers* Ⅲ 🍴 🍸 🖥️ 🎾 ≋ ✂️ ▦ ★ ☘️ 📺 800/996-3426

This hotel, decked out in hardwood and beige from the marble lobby to the spacious rooms, is an oasis of intimacy. Many guests return year after year to find the same staff members who know them by name. The views from the rooftop pool, and health club – of city lights and nearby Bunker Hill – are breathtaking, and the Checkers Restaurant is consistently rated one of the finest in town.

The Regal Biltmore Hotel (3)
506 S. Grand Avenue, Los Angeles, CA 90071 ☎ 213/624-1011

(5th St.) Ⓜ *Pershing Square* 🅿️ 🈁 *693 rooms (15 suites)* ●● ▭ ⏰ ▣ 🈂️ 🏧 Ⅲ 🍴 *Smeraldi's, Sai Sai* 🍸 *Gallery, Grand Avenue* 🖥️ *Biltmore Bakery* 🏪 *Club Lounge* 🎾 🏊 ♨️ ✚ ≋ ✂️ ▦ ☘️ 📺 800/245-8673

This 1923 Spanish-Italian renaissance-style building was the home to some of the first Oscar ceremonies. Rooms are cozy and well-appointed with overstuffed chairs and plush draperies, and the Biltmore Club floor features larger rooms, special services for business travelers and a dedicated staff.

Hotel Figueroa (4)
939 S. Figueroa Street, Los Angeles, CA 90015 ☎ 213/627-8971

(9th St.) Ⓜ *7th St.* 🅿️ *285 rooms (2 suites)* ●● ▭ ⏰ 🈂️ 🏧 Ⅲ 🍴 *Pasta Firenze, Music Room* 🍸 *Veranda* 🎾 ♨️ ≋ ▦ ★ ☘️ 📺 800/421-9092

Deep reds, browns, blues and pastels make up this 1927 hotel's eclectic tilework, murals and tapestries. Wrought-iron beds and beamed ceilings round out the large rooms, and meals can be taken in the tropical poolside garden.

Not forgetting

■ **Hotel Inter-Continental Los Angeles at California Plaza (5)** 251 S. Olive St., Los Angeles, CA 90012 ☎ 213/617-3300 ●●●● *Stylishly modern with a sculpture garden in the lobby, and large rooms decorated in appealing California colors* ■ **New Otani Hotel (6)** 120 S. Los Angeles St., Los Angeles, CA 90000 ☎ 213/629-1200 ●●● *LA branch of large Japanese chain. Famous third-floor Japanese garden with waterfalls and ponds, and highly regarded Japanese restaurants.* ■ **Miyako Inn (7)** 328 E. 1st St., Los Angeles, CA 90012 ☎ 213/617-2000 ●● *Popular with businessmen, this hotel in Little Tokyo has western-style rooms and a karaoke lounge.*

16

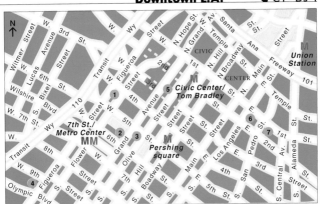

The original center of Los Angeles and still a hub of business and culture, Downtown is undergoing a renaissance with large additions including the Convention Center, Staples Center sports arena, and the upcoming Walt Disney Concert Hall.

In the area

- **Where to eat:** ➡ 42 ➡ 56
- **After dark:** ➡ 78
- **What to see:** ➡86 ➡ 92
- **Where to shop:** ➡ 130

➡ Where to stay

Saga Motel (8)
1633 E. Colorado Blvd, Pasadena, CA 91101 ☎ 626/795-0431

(Sierra Bonita) **P** *70 rooms* ● 🏢 ▭ ▣ 📷 Ⅲ 🎞 🎿 ✖ **TV** *800/793-7242*

Not only can you cruise down Route 66 (a.k.a. Pasadena's Colorado Boulevard), you can also sleep there, at this motel that has existed since that historic road was the main route to the West Coast. Rooms at this Mom & Pop operation have photos of early local history, and the friendly staff goes out of its way to make sure you're taken care of.

Ritz Carlton Huntington Hotel & Spa (9)
1401 S. Oak Knoll Avenue, Pasadena, CA 91106 ☎ 626/568-3900

(Alpine St.) **P** 🏊 *392 rooms (26 suites)* ●●●● ▭ 🕐 ▣ 📷 ▐ Ⅲ 🏛 *The Terrace, The Grill* **Y** *The Bar* 🍸 *The Lobby Lounge* 🍴 🎿 🎞 ✚ 🎿 🎾 ⊞ ✖ 🥅 **TV** *800/241-3333*

A great Southern California classic, this 1906 estate atop a hill has 23 acres of palatial gardens. Old-world style guest rooms are awash in dusty blue and sage green. Together with California's first Olympic-sized pool and a beauty salon, the spa boasts several types of massage and treatments including champagne facials. And just so you don't forget where you are, there are grand views of distant Los Angeles from the lounge.

Bissell House B & B (10)
201 Orange Grove Ave, South Pasadena, CA 91030 ☎ 626/441-3535

(Columbia Ave) **P** *5 rooms (1 suite)* ●● 🏢 ▭ Ⅲ 🎞 ✚ 🎿 ✖ 🥅 **TV** *800/441-3530*

'Millionaires' Row' was long the destination for Midwestern society folk seeking sun and relaxation. One such heiress was Anna Bissell McCay, the daughter of Melville Bissell of carpet sweeper fame, and now her 1887 house has opened to the public. Decorated with Victorian antiques and photos of both the Bissell family and the current owners.

Artist's Inn B & B (11)
1038 Magnolia St., South Pasadena, CA 91030 ☎ 626/799-56681

(Fairview) **P** *9 rooms (3 suites)* ●● 🏢 ▭ ▣ 📷 Ⅲ 🎿 🎞 **TV** *888/799-5668* @ *artistsinn@artistsinn.com*

A warm staff make this one-time farmhouse pleasurable and a neighborhood of well-kept homes has filled in the former fields, making it a great place to experience small-town America. Rooms are decorated in tribute to Van Gogh, Gauguin, Grandma Moses and the Impressionists, among others, and on the ample front lawn with its garden of 100 rose bushes, croquet is encouraged.

Not forgetting

■ **Doubletree Hotel** (12) 191 N. Los Robbles Ave, Pasadena, CA 91101 ☎ 626/792-2727 ●●● *Friendly, welcoming full-service hotel with separate concierge floor and a health club.* ■ **Pasadena Hilton** (13) 150 S. Los Robbles Ave, Pasadena, CA 91101 ☎ 626/577-1000 ●●● *Hardwood, marble and skylights create a tone of understated elegance, and a sports bar rounds out the lobby of this 1971 hotel.*

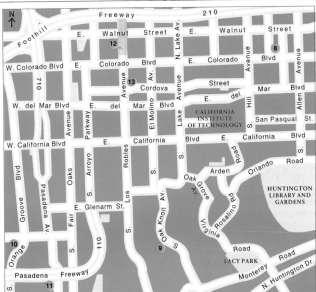

In L.A. but not part of it, Pasadena is known for gracious Southern California living, with stately homes, excellent museums [➡92] and the Rose Bowl stadium. The 1990s boom in the Old Town district made this once-staid city into a real destination, with lodgings that are bargains compared to elsewhere in town.

Where to stay

Hollywood Hills Magic Hotel (14)
7025 Franklin Avenue, Los Angeles, CA 90028 ☎ 323/851-0800

(Sycamore Dr.) Ⓜ *Hollywood* 🅿 *43 rooms (40 suites)* ● 🔲 🖥 📷 🎚 🎽 ≋
⭐ 🧹 📺 *800/741-4915* @ *info@magichotel.com*

Although it faces busy Franklin Avenue, the atmosphere inside this
converted apartment building is quiet, bright and cloistered around a
central pool. Built into the hillside, most rooms are one-bedroom
apartment suites, comfortable if not fancy. The hotel borrows its name
from the Magic Castle, the magicians' club just up the hill, for which the
staff can arrange tickets for hotel guests.

Orange Drive Manor (15)
1764 N. Orange Drive, Los Angeles, CA 90028 ☎ 323/850-0350

(between Franklin Ave and Hollywood Blvd) Ⓜ *Hollywood* 🅿 *43 rooms* ● 🗐 ⭐

Although it's surrounded by busy Hollywood, an atmosphere of peace
prevails in this 1920s mansion turned youth hostel. It doesn't have any big
hotel amenities (or even a sign out in front), but knowledgeable budget
travelers swear by it. Dormitory-style rooms and single/double rooms are
available.

Orchid Suites Hotel (16)
1753 N. Orchid Avenue, Los Angeles, CA 90028 ☎ 323/874-9678

(between Franklin Ave and Hollywood Blvd) Ⓜ *Hollywood* 🅿 *40 rooms*
(16 suites) ● 🎦 🔲 🖥 📷 🎚 🏓 🎽 ≋ ⭐ 🧹 📺 *800/537-3052*
@ *info@orchidsuites.com*

The large rooms in this small hotel are well appointed with full kitchens,
balconies or patios, and the hosts are jovial. You can take your breakfast
either in the lobby or by the pool in the bright central courtyard. It's
conveniently located adjacent to the Academy Theater.

Hollywood Roosevelt Hotel (17)
7000 Hollywood Boulevard, Los Angeles, CA 90028 ☎ 323/466-7000

(N. Orange Dr.) Ⓜ *Hollywood* 🅿 🗓 *335 rooms (35 suites)* ●● 🔲 🖥 📷 🛗
🎚 🍴 *Theodore's* 🍸 *Teddy's* 🍽 *Grand Central Café* 🏓 🗙 🎽 ✚ ≋
🏓 ⊞ 🥂 *Cinegrill* 🧹 📺 *800/950-7667* @ *sales@hollywoodroosevelt.com*

This 1927 landmark, home to the first Academy Awards ceremony,
remains a classic, even if rooms were renovated in 2000 with Harlequin
colors and fanciful designs. You can almost imagine stars of yesteryear
mingling in the Spanish-style lobby – the ghosts of Marilyn Monroe and
Montgomery Clift are said to make occasional appearances – and for
generations the Cinegrill lounge has been one of L.A.'s best venues for
cabaret singers. Be sure also to check out the exhibit in the mezzanine,
on Hollywood history from 1886 to 1945.

Not forgetting
■ **Highland Gardens Hotel (18)** 7047 Franklin Ave, Los Angeles,
CA 90028 ☎ 323/850-0536 ● *The vast apartments, some with their own
kitchens, look out over a lush inner garden featuring a swimming pool.*

Hollywood had fallen on hard times in the late 20th century, but there are big expectations for its future, thanks to a comprehensive Times Square-style makeover, including the new theater for the Academy Awards ceremony. Many Hollywood hotels are now relatively inexpensive, but that could all change in a couple of years.

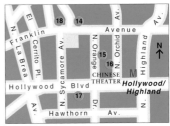

17

17

18

18

In the area

- **Where to eat:** ➟ 46 ➟ 48
- **After dark:** ➟ 68 ➟ 72 ➟ 74 ➟ 76 ➟ 78 ➟ 82
- **What to see:** ➟ 86 ➟ 102
- **Where to shop:** ➟ 136

Where to stay

The Argyle (19)
8358 Sunset Blvd, West Hollywood, CA 90069 ☎ 323/654-7100

(Sweetzer Ave) 🅿 🛗 *64 rooms (44 suites)* ●●●● ▢ Ⓞ ▣ ☎ ▥ ▥ ▥
▥ Fenix Ⓨ ▥ ➕ ▥ ▥ ★ ▥ ▥ 800/225-2637 @ rez@argylehotel.com

Art-Deco splendor and amazing city views are two of the hallmarks of this
1931 landmark. The jewelbox rooms have sitting areas and marble bathrooms with black-and-white fixtures. The poolside Fenix restaurant is highly
regarded for its California cuisine with Cajun touches. You may recognize
the hotel from 'The Player' – it's where Tim Robbins exits the cozy
driveway… and finds that symbol of Hollywood – a snake – in his car.

⭐ The Standard (20)
8300 Sunset Blvd, West Hollywood, CA 90069 ☎ 323/650-9090

(Sweetzer Ave) 🅿 🛗 *138 rooms (2 suites)* ●● ▢ Ⓞ ▣ ☎ ▥ ▥ ▥ ▥ Ⓨ ▥
▥ ▥ ▤ ★ ▥

This recently-opened bargain on the Strip has its tongue firmly planted
in its cheek and an Austin Powers-mod style (bubble chairs, thick shag
carpeting on the lobby floor, walls and ceiling). Check out the cobalt
blue astroturf poolside and great views, the barbershop/tattoo parlor
and the room fans which read 'blow, hard, harder, stop' in place of 'low,
medium, high, off'. The restaurant is the new hotspot for hipsters.

Mondrian (21)
8440 Sunset Blvd, West Hollywood, CA 90069 ☎ 323/650-8999

(Olive Dr.) 🅿 🛗 *238 rooms (187 suites)* ●●●●● ▢ Ⓞ ▣ ☎ ▥ ▥ ▥ Asia
de Cuba Ⓨ Sky Bar ➟ 72 ▥ ▤ ▨ ➕ ▥ ▥ ★ ▥ ▥ 800/525-8029

Ian Schrager (of New York's Royalton and Miami's Delano) has made this
Sunset Strip establishment his beachhead on the West Coast. Every
doorman and desk clerk could be a model in this fun and wily hotel with
oversize flower pots, three-story doors to nowhere and a poolside that
can only be described as a scene. The Asia de Cuba restaurant and Sky
Bar are still among the hottest reservations in town (yes, reservations
for a bar), but hotel guests get special treatment.

Not forgetting
■ **Sunset Marquis Hotel & Villas (22)** 1200 Alta Loma Rd, West
Hollywood, CA 90069 ☎ 213/624-1011 ●●●● *A civilized oasis. Rooms in the
main building have garden or hillside views, and the villas are popular with music
industry guests – there's a recording studio on the premises. As a guest you'll be
able to get into the ultra-hip Whisky Bar.* ■ **Le Parc Suite Hotel (23)**
8822 Cynthia St., West Hollywood, CA 90069 ☎ 310/855-8888 ●●●●● *This
former apartment building is all suites and big enough to have a tennis court on
the roof.* ■ **Le Reve Hotel (24)** 8822 Cynthia St., West Hollywood, CA
90069 ☎ 310/854-1114 ●● *On a quiet street with two-level suites this French
country-style hotel has a rooftop pool with city and hill views.* ■ **Chateau
Marmont (25)** 8221 Sunset Blvd, Hollywood, CA 90046 ☎ 323/656-1010
●●● *Large celebrity clientele at this small 1920s hotel that looks like a
Normandy castle.* ■ **Ramada West Hollywood (26)** 8585 Santa Monica
Blvd, West Hollywood, CA 90069 ☎ 213/617-2000 ●● *Awash in white, this is
the only hotel on the Boys' Town strip.* ■ **San Vicente Inn (27)** 845 N. San
Vicente Blvd, West Hollywood, CA 90069 ☎ 310/854-6915 ●●

The Sunset Strip is one of America's best-known streets, and a quick look at these hotels will tell you why. Down the hill, West Hollywood 'Boys' Town', along Santa Monica Boulevard, is a Mecca for gay visitors from around the world.

In the area
Where to eat: ➥ 50 ➥ 52 ➥ 56
After dark: ➥ 70 ➥ 72
What to see: ➥ 86 ➥ 102
Where to shop: ➥ 126 ➥ 140 ➥ 142

Where to stay

Beverly Hills Hotel (28)

9641 Sunset Blvd, Beverly Hills, CA 90210 ☎ 310/276-2251

(Crescent Dr.) ***203 rooms (27 suites 22 bungalows)*** ●●●●● *The Polo Lounge* *The Fountain Coffee Shop* *The Sunset Lounge* *800/283-8885*

Aficionados of this fabled 1919 pink palace swear by the one-of-a-kind bungalows, and suites of up to 4 bedrooms with fireplaces, balconies and marble and gilt bathrooms. It has lush gardens and the sort of cabana-lined swimming pool that makes everyone want to move to California. Check out the friendly coffee shop counter in the basement, and don't forget to drop by the legendary Polo Lounge restaurant.

Regent Beverly Wilshire (29)

9500 Wilshire Blvd, Beverly Hills, CA 90212 ☎ 310/275-5200

(between Rodeo and Beverly Drs) ***396 rooms (120 suites)*** ●●●●● *The Lobby Lounge, The Dining Room* *The Lobby Lounge* *800/421-4354*

The Grande Dame of Beverly Hills hotels; rooms were renovated for the millennium with muted golds and grays, and walnut trim, glass shower stalls and deep bathtubs in the marble bathrooms. Once you see it, you'll know why Richard Gere took Julia Roberts here in the movie 'Pretty Woman'.

Penninsula Beverly Hills (30)

9882 Little Santa Monica Blvd, Beverly Hills, CA 90212 ☎ 310/551-2888

(Wilshire Blvd) ***164 rooms (32 suites 16 villas)*** ●●●●● *The Belvedere* *The Club Bar* *The Roof Garden* *The Living Room* *800/462-7899* *pbh@penninsula.com*

This luxurious four-story hotel has generous-sized rooms in muted tans and pinks with many personal touches; there is a rooftop garden with a spa and 60-foot heated outdoor pool overlooking Beverly Hills and Century City; in the lush gardens are villas with one and two bedrooms.

Not forgetting

■ **L'Ermitage (31)** 9291 Burton Way, Beverly Hills, CA 90210 ☎ 310/ 278-3344 ●●●●● *Light gray and pale English sycamore create a mood of subtle Asian-style elegance.* ■ **Avalon (32)** 9400 Olympic Blvd, Beverly Hills, CA 90212 ☎ 310/277-5221 ●●● *Renovated in 1999 with period furnishings by Heywood Wakefield, Eames and Noguchi. A rooftop Zen garden and in-room acupuncture.* ■ **Renaissance Beverly Hills (33)** 1224 S. Beverly Dr., Los Angeles, CA 90035 ☎ 310/277- 2800 ●●●● *This high-rise at the base of Rodeo Drive offers warm, personal service and sweeping views. The upper 'concierge floors' have business services, a private bar and their own staff.* ■ **Four Seasons Beverly Hills (34)** 300 S. Doheny Dr., Los Angeles, CA 90048 ☎ 310/273-2222 ●●● *True first-level hotel, known for caring staff and attention to detail.* ■ **Beverly Hilton (35)** 9876 Wilshire Blvd, Beverly Hills, CA 90212 ☎ 310/274-7777 ●●●● *Most rooms have balconies, and sleek lobby features striking fountains and a full supply of shops ➥ 143 Trader Vic's, the tony Polynesian bar, seems to never go out of style ➥ 70.* ■ **Beverly Hills Inn (36)** 125 S. Spalding Dr., Beverly Hills, CA 90212 ●● ☎ 310/278-0303 *Charming European style hotel with many big-hotel amenities (exercise room, heated pool, happy hour).*

Many of the hotels in the area are rated very high internationally, adding to the aura of luxury surrounding Beverly Hills. However, new and rather more modest establishments have great surprises in store.

4

34   29

Where to stay

Bel-Air Hotel (37)
701 Stone Canyon Road, Los Angeles, CA 90077 ☎ 310/472-1211

(Sunset Blvd) 🅿 🍽 **92 rooms (40 suites)** ●●●●● ▢ ▢ ▢ ▢ ▢ ▢ ▢ 🍴 *The Restaurant* ➡ 46 ▢ ▢ ▢ ▢ ▢ ▢ ▢ ▢ ▢ ▢ ▢

This hotel, opened in 1946, is perfect for romantics. Winding paths make their way through the lush greenery of the grounds, among the ornamental pools and their gliding swans. You would think you were out in the countryside and not in the second-largest metropolis in America. Some rooms come with a fireplace, and the staff will be happy to light a fire for you. The concierges are famous for their many talents, and the restaurant is one of the best in L.A.

Luxe Summit Hotel Bel-Air (38)
11461 Sunset Blvd, Los Angeles, CA 90049 ☎ 310/476-6571

(Church Lane) 🅿 🍽 **162 rooms (58 suites)** ●●● ▢ ▢ ▢ ▢ ▢ ▢ ▢ ▢ 🍴 *Cafe Bel-Air* ▢ ▢ ▢ ▢ ▢ ▢ ▢ ▢ ▢ ▢ ▢ ▢ 800/468-3541

These two contemporary buildings are havens of tranquility nestling on the hillside in a verdant setting. Many rooms look out over the city or the Getty Center, to which there is a regular shuttle service provided by the hotel. The establishment often plays host to stars from the sport and entertainment worlds, but the staff shows no favoritism.

W (39)
930 Hilgard Avenue, Los Angeles, CA 90024 ☎ 310/208-8765

(Le Conte Ave) 🍽 **280 suites** ●●●● ▢ ▢ ▢ ▢ ▢ ▢ ▢ ▢ 🍴 *Mojo* ▢ ▢ ▢ ▢ ▢ ▢ ▢ ▢ ▢ ▢ ▢ 877/946-8357

A high-rise that thinks of itself as a boutique, offering large, stylish suites with pillow-top mattresses, down comforters, sweeping city views and a host of in-room gadgets, and staff who introduce themselves to each guest to ensure personal service. The black, pale-green and gray color scheme is cool but not cold. There are not one but two pools, and the lobby is designed as a comfortable game room.

Century Wilshire Hotel (40)
10776 Wilshire Blvd, Los Angeles, CA 90024 ☎ 310/474-4506

(between Malcolm and Selby) 🅿 **99 rooms (60 suites)** ●● ▢ ▢ ▢ ▢ ▢ ▢ ▢ ▢ 800/421-7223 @ cwhotel@aol.com

This quaint, unpretentious European-style hotel in a converted apartment building sits around a lovely courtyard with blue and white awnings. While not luxurious, the rooms are large, and many have kitchens; there's a bright, comfortable pool area out back.

Not forgetting

■ **Holiday Inn Brentwood (41)** 170 N. Church Lane, Los Angeles, CA 90049 ☎ 310/476-6411 ●●● *Most of the rooms have a view over the ocean or the city. Ask for the more peaceful, ocean-view rooms.* ■ **Hilgard House (42)** 927 Hilgard Avenue, Los Angeles, CA 90024 ☎ 310/208-3945 ● *Early American-style furnishings and well-stocked bookcases lend an academic feel to this intimate 3-story building at the edge of the UCLA campus* ➡ 104.

These districts – commonly known as the Westside or West L.A. – suddenly became hot again in the late 1990s, as the Getty Center moved to Brentwood and UCLA-adjacent Westwood began its resurgence as a dining and entertainment destination. Its hotels – both new and old – have kept pace.

37

39

37

39

Where to stay

Channel Road Inn (43)
219 West Channel Rd, Santa Monica, CA 90402 ☎ 310/459-1920

(Pacific Coast Highway) 🅿 *14 rooms (2 suites)* ●●● ▢ ▣ ▢ ▥ ▩ ▨ ✦ ❄ @ *channelinn@aol.com*

New England bed & breakfast in a Craftsman building (Santa Monica's signature style). Friendly communal areas include the comfortable breakfast room and the Jacuzzi (well, this is California), and you can even use the hotel's bikes to tour Santa Monica Canyon or the ocean bike path.

Hotel Oceana (44)
849 Ocean Avenue, Santa Monica, CA 90403 ☎ 310/393-0486

(Montana Ave) 🏨 *63 suites* ●●●●● ▢ ▣ ▢ ▢ ▢ ▣ ▥ ▩ ❄ ✱ ✦ ❄ ▽ 800/777-0758 @ *beachsuite@aol.com*

The luxurious suites are inspired by the French Riviera, with walls of cobalt blue and deep yellow, Frette bed linens, large marble bathrooms and vanities, dining areas and kitchens stocked with gourmet pizzas. But it's the intimate poolside courtyard and eager staff that give this hotel its real charm. Many rooms overlook the Pacific, or at least Palisades Park across the street.

Fairmont Miramar (45)
101 Wilshire Blvd, Santa Monica, CA 90401 ☎ 310/576-7777

(Ocean Blvd) 🅿 🏨 *302 rooms (61 suites)* ●●●●● ▢ ▢ ▣ ▢ ▢ ▥ ❚❚❚ *The Grill, The Cafe* ▽ ▩ ▨ ▨ ✱ ❄ ▨ ▦ ✦ ❄ ▽ 800/4866-5577

A favorite of heads-of-state, entertainment figures and businesspeople since the cozy original bungalows opened on this site in 1889, as evidenced by photos of famous guests throughout. Today the refurbished bungalows, next to the lush garden and pool, feature hardwood floors and umbrellas to escort you back to the main building on those rare rainy days. Slightly larger rooms have balconies with views.

Not forgetting

■ **Shangri-La (46)** 1301 Ocean Ave, Santa Monica, CA 90401 ☎ 310/627-8971 ●● *This 1939 Art-Deco Streamline-Moderne building has many rooms that are suites with kitchens and retro furnishings, and penthouses have 360-degree ocean, hill and mountain views.* ■ **The Georgian (47)** 1415 Ocean Ave, Santa Monica, CA 90401 ☎ 310/395-9945 ●●●● *You can almost imagine old-time celebrities such as Gable & Lombard and mobster Bugsy Siegel in this sea-blue-façaded Art-Deco gem they frequented. The front veranda offers excellent people watching and ocean views.* ■ **Hosteling International Youth Hostel (48)** 1432 2nd St., Santa Monica, CA 90401 ☎ 310/393-9913 ● *Possibly the youth hostel with the best location in the world. Dormitory rooms for ten and double rooms; no private bathrooms but sheets are included.* ■ **Cal Mar Suites & Hotel (49)** 220 California Ave, Santa Monica, CA 90401 ☎ 310/395-5555 ●● *This discreet hotel offers all suites looking out over the central swimming pool.* ■ **Radisson Huntley Hotel (50)** 1111 2nd St., Santa Monica, CA 90403 ☎ 310/394-5454 ●●● *High-rise with Georgian-style carpentry and ocean views from comfortable rooms. The glass express elevator to the rooftop Topper's restaurant is Santa Monica's best thrill ride.* ■ **Hotel Carmel (51)** 201 Broadway, Santa Monica, CA 90401 ☎ 310/451-2469 ●● *Dating from 1924, this hotel is basic but comfortable and well kept.*

In the 1990s, this city transformed itself from the 'People's
Republic of Santa Monica' into
'Beverly Hills by the Sea', and
now the shopping, dining and
entertainment options make it
one of the most sought-after
locations.

46

HOTEL
SHANGRI·LA

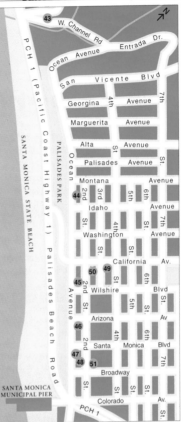

W. Channel Rd
43

Ocean Avenue Entrada Dr.

PCH 1 (Pacific Coast Highway 1)

San Vicente Blvd

Georgina Avenue 4th 7th

Marguerita Avenue

Alta St. Avenue

Palisades Avenue St.

Ocean Avenue

PALISADES PARK

SANTA MONICA STATE BEACH

Montana Avenue
44 2nd 3rd 5th 6th

Idaho Avenue
St. 4th St. 7th

Washington Avenue
St. St.

California Av.
50 **49** St. 6th

Wilshire Blvd
45 2nd St. 5th St.

Arizona Av
46 2nd 4th 6th

Santa Monica Blvd
47 St. 7th

Broadway
48 **51** St. St. St. St.

SANTA MONICA
MUNICIPAL PIER

Colorado Av.
PCH 1 St.

Palisades Beach Road

Avenue

43

44

43

51

In the area

 Where to eat: ➡ 56 ➡ 60
After dark: ➡ 68 ➡ 70 ➡ 74 ➡ 80
What to see: ➡ 86 ➡ 96 ➡ 106 ➡ 108
Where to shop: ➡ 126 ➡ 144

▶ Where to stay

Hotel California (52)
1670 Ocean Avenue, Santa Monica, CA 90401 ☎ 310/393-2363

(between Colorado Ave and Pico Blvd) 🅿 **26 rooms (6 suites)** ●● ▣ ▣ ▣ ▨
✪ ☑ 800/537-8483 @ info@hotelca.com

Admittedly this motel isn't the *Hotel California* of the Eagles' song. It is nevertheless a pleasant and fun alternative to its opulent neighbors, a sort of 'bed and breakfast without the breakfast' in the words of the staff. Painted surfboards and colorful antique tiles decorate the exterior. The cozy rooms with their wooden floors come with refrigerators.

Hotel Casa del Mar (53)
1910 Ocean Front Walk, Santa Monica, CA 90405 ☎ 310/581-5533

(Appian Way) 🅿 ▥ **129 rooms (20 suites)** ●●●●● ▣ ⏻ ▣ ▣ ▥ ▥ ▥
▥ Oceanfront ▼ The Lounge ▧ ▨ ✚ ≋ ▧ ▦ ▨ ☑ 800/898-6999
@ reservations@hotelcasadelmar.com

From the sweeping, tiled foyer staircase to the opulent lobby and perfect beachside views, the 1999 renovation of this 1926 landmark was done flawlessly. Bathrooms feature individual Jacuzzis and playful peek-a-boo windows to the bedrooms, known for their comfortable beds. A worthy sister property to Shutters, across the street.

Cadillac Hotel (54)
8 Dudley Avenue, Venice, CA 90291 ☎ 310/399-8876

(between Speedway and Ocean Front Walk) 🅿 **40 rooms (5 suites)** ● ▣ ▣ ▣
▥ ▧ ✪ ▨ @ cadillac@deltanet.com

Another of Chaplin's one-time residences, this Art-Deco building, steps from the beach, has been restored with an intimate, modern and quirky feel. Its bright colored lobby lounge doubles as a game room, with a pool table and a chunk of the Berlin Wall.

Not forgetting

■ **The Venice Beach House (55)** 15 Thirtieth Ave, Venice, CA 90291 ☎ 310/823-1966 ●● *Every suite tells a story – of the pier, or the tramp (Charlie Chaplin, who once lived here) – in this turn-of-the-last-century craftsman-style bed and breakfast.* ■ **Le Merigot Beach Hotel (56)** 1740 Ocean Ave, Santa Monica, CA 90401 ☎ 213/627-8971 ●●●●● *Its fortress-like façade belies its charms – a friendly staff and spacious rooms with plush bedding, and mostly wonderful views.* ■ **Shutters on the Beach (57)** 1 Pico Blvd, Santa Monica, CA 90405 ☎ 310/459-0030 ●●●●● *This plantation-style hotel on the beach sets the standard for luxury with elegantly decorated rooms, a pool, and its artwork – of artists such as David Hockney; its One Pico Restaurant overlooks the ocean.* ■ **Loews Santa Monica Beach Hotel (58)** 1700 Ocean Ave, Santa Monica, CA 90401 ☎ 310/458-6700 ●●●●● *The hotel won many architectural awards when it first opened in 1989, and it received a facelift in 2000 including four-story palms in the atrium lobby. The hotel's Lavande restaurant, with its ocean views, is considered one of Santa Monica's finest.* ■ **Marina Pacific Hotel (59)** 1697 Pacific Ave, Venice, CA 90291 ☎ 310/452-1111 ●● *Many of the large rooms, in sand and surf tones, have balconies with partial ocean views. Quiet at the heart of bustling Venice.*

LOEW
SANTA MONIC
BEACH HOTE

Last year the southern end of Santa Monica suddenly became one of L.A.'s busiest hotel districts, with three new or renovated properties opening within a few months of each other. Venice accommodations put you squarely in the middle of that district's funky charm.

Where to stay

Barnabey's Hotel (60)
3501 Sepulveda Blvd, Manhattan Beach, CA 90266 ☎ 310/545-8466

(Rosecrans Ave) 🅿 🚭 *121 rooms* ●● ▭ 🕐 ▣ ☎ ⫼ 🎏 *Auberge Restaurant* 🍸 *Barnabey's Pub* 🐕 ❌ 〰 ❌ ⊞ ◉ ✱ 📺 *800/552-5285*

The interior of this charming hotel is more London than Los Angeles – almost more London than London – with antique furnishings, canopy beds, Victorian and Edwardian prints, nautical paintings, towel warmers, and lace and floral patterns throughout. This being California, though, there's also a lush semitropical garden around the pool, and rooms in this area have balconies. They also offer shuttle service to LAX.

Sea View Inn (61)
3400 Highland Ave, Manhattan Beach, CA 90266 ☎ 310/545-1504

(34th St.) 🅿 *19 rooms (2 suites)* ● ▭ ▣ ☎ ⫼ 🚳 〰 ❌ ✱ 🍴

A collection of small buildings, the Sea View is just steps from the beach and surrounded by Manhattan Beach's spirited nightlife. The rooms may not be fancy, but they are comfortable with refrigerators and apartment-style bathrooms, and many have balconies or courtyard settings. The friendly staff will provide beach towels and chairs, as well as bikes for the bike path. If you're sensitive to noise, request a room away from busy Highland Avenue.

Sea Sprite Hotel (62)
1016 The Strand, Hermosa Beach, CA 90254 ☎ 213/627-8971

(10ᵗʰ St.) 🅿 *70 rooms (15 suites)* ● ▭ ▣ ☎ 🚳 〰 ✱ 🍴

No restaurant, no deluxe rooms, no pillow chocolates … no problem. When your reasonably priced room is right on the beach and a block from Hermosa's best dining and shopping, it's hard to complain. Apartment-style furnishings include kitchens in many of the rooms.

Portofino Hotel & Yacht Club (63)
260 Portofino Way, Redondo Beach, CA 90277 ☎ 310/379-8481

(Harbor Dr.) 🅿 *163 rooms (2 suites)* ●●● ▭ ▣ ☎ 🛗 ⫼ 🎏 *Pooch's* 🍸 🐕 🚳 ✿ 〰 ❌ ✱ 🍴 📺 *800/468-4292* @ *portofinosales@compuserve.com*

The ocean views to one side, down to the Palos Verdes Peninsula and Catalina Island, and yacht harbor sights and sounds on the other lull you into a state of tranquility at this modern hotel, the South Bay's only luxury property. All rooms have private decks, and the Pooch's restaurant is one of the area's finest for Italian specialties, despite its downmarket name.

Not forgetting

■ **Palos Verdes Inn (64)** 1700 S. Pacific Coast Highway, Redondo Beach, CA 90277 ☎ 310/316-4211 ●● *Large sundeck and indoor/outdoor heated pool. Clean, basic rooms, many with bay or hill views.*

The cities of Manhattan Beach, Hermosa Beach and Redondo Beach are known for their laid-back lifestyle, surf, sun and outdoor activities. After all, this is the area that gave the world the Beach Boys.

63

EL PORTO

61

Rosecrans Avenue

31st St.

60

Marine Av.

Highland Av.

Bell Av.

Valley Dr.

Ardmore Avenue

Marine Av.

Pacific Avenue

MANHATTAN
BEACH PIER Manhattan

Beach Boulevard

9th Poinsettia

Manhattan Avenue

N. Highland

N. Manhattan

MANHATTAN
BEACH

HERMOSA
BEACH

Valley Av.

Ardmore Av.

N. 2nd Street

Sepulveda

S. Meadows

HERMOSA
BEACH

Monterey Dr.

Valley

Ardmore

Highway

Artesia Blvd

S. Peck Av.

Beach Avenue

Pier Av.

Prospect Av.

Harper Av.

Ford Av.

Blvd

62

Coast

Aviation

Pacific Avenue

Hermosa

6th Street

Prospect

Herondo St.

Anita Av.

St.

KING
HARBOR

N. Harbor Dr.

Highway Avenue

Street

63

Beryl

REDONDO
BEACH

Catalina

Diamond St.

Pacific Coast

Vincent St.

Prospect Av.

N. Pacific

Garnet St.

Torrance Blvd

BEACH

Highway

Camino Real

REDONDO COUNTY

Esplanade

Coast

Avenue A

Camino Real

Catalina Avenue

Pacific

Avenue C

Avenue Av.

Verdes Blvd

S. Catalina

S. Gertruda Av.

Palos

Prospect

Susana Av.

64

Verdes Blvd

Pacific Coast

HOLLYWOOD
RIVIERA

Palos

Calle Mayor

Calle Mayor

TORRANCE

Where to stay

Lord Mayor's Inn (65)
435 Cedar Street, Long Beach, CA 90802 ☎ 562/436-0324

(5th St.) Ⓜ *Pacific Ave* 🅿 *13 rooms* ● 🗹 ▭ ✪ @ *innkeepers@lordmayor's.com*

Built in 1904, this elegant Edwardian building was the residence of the first mayor of the town, Charles H. Windham. It has now been turned into a bed and breakfast. Laura and Reuben Brasser, the landlords, make their guests feel at home with their warm welcome. Their careful restoration work earned them the Long Beach 'Preservationist of the Year' award in 1999. The rooms, such as Margarita's Room (formerly that of the Mayor's daughter), are furnished true to period. Over the years, the house annexed two other 1906 buildings, Apple House and Cinnamon House, very practical for families who want their own living space.

Inn of Long Beach (66)
185 Atlantic Avenue, Long Beach, CA 90802 ☎ 562/435-3791

(Broadway) 🅿 *45 rooms (1 suite)* ● 🗹 ▭ ▣ 🖾 Ⅲ ▨
🕎 *800/230-7500*

The rhythms of late 1960s architecture are set off nicely against the good-size pool and Jacuzzi area of this informal, friendly inn. While not fancy, the rooms are spacious and comfortable, and all have decks or balconies facing the courtyard and refrigerators you can stock yourself. There's also shuttle service to many city attractions.

Dockside Boat & Bed (67)
Dock 5, Rainbow Harbor, Long Beach, CA 90802 ☎ 562/436-3111

(Pine Ave) 🅿 *3 cabins* ●● 🗹 ▭ ▣ 🖾 ✗ 🕎 *800-4-DOCKSIDE*
@ *boatandbed@aol.com*

OK, so it's not the *Queen Mary*, but this comfortable outlet will allow you to stay on board luxury motor or sailing yachts that sleep up to 8. The inventory of boats changes frequently, so if they don't have what you want, just ask – the agreeable staff may just be able to get it for you. Shopping and restaurants are available at Shoreline Village, a short walk away, and if you want to take the boats out, they'll even arrange for a captain.

Queen Mary (68)
1126 Queens Highway, Long Beach, CA 90802 ☎ 562/435-3511

🅿 🕅 *367 cabins (8 suites)* ●● ▭ ▣ 🖾 Ⅲ 🏬 *Sir Winston's* ➡ 64,
The Chelsea, The Promenade Cafe 🕎 *The Lobby Bar* ▣ ✕ 🕏 ✚ ✕ ⊞
◉ *The Observation Bar* 🕎 *800/437-2934*

Who hasn't dreamed of spending the night on an ocean liner, even if she never leaves the dock? The *Queen Mary*, launched in 1934, was the largest liner ever built and a showcase of Art-Deco luxury. It has 367 cabins and 8 suites that you can rent by the night and most of them have retained their original furnishings and those luxury gadgets that make a cruise an unforgettable adventure. A veritable floating town, the ship offers numerous services: restaurants, activities and stores that will be more than enough to fill the day.

Once a sleepy beach town, Long Beach has recently been drawing in crowds thanks to the *Queen Mary*, the Aquarium of the Pacific ➥ 110, nightlife along busy Pine Avenue and its large convention center.

➡ Where to eat

Dine with the stars?
With a bit of luck you will find your favorite star dining at one of these establishments.

The Restaurant ➡ 46
Chinois on Main ➡ 58
Crustacean ➡ 50
KoKoMo ➡ 52
Lucques ➡ 48
Maple Drive ➡ 50
Matsuhisa ➡ 48
Nate 'n' Al's ➡ 50
Musso & Frank Grill ➡ 44
Patina ➡ 44
Pink's Hot Dog ➡ 44
Spago Beverly Hills ➡ 50

Prices
The prices given in this guide represent the average per person cost of a 3-course meal (appetizer, main course, dessert), excluding beverages, tax and tip.

Tips
Your tip should be between 15% and 20% of the bill or twice the tax (8.25%). If you are paying by credit card, write the amount of the tip under the total sum payable; add it up and sign.

Californian cuisine

Los Angeles' culinary scene reflects the diverse nature of its population and is strongly influenced by it. Since the 1970s, the city's restaurants have been in the forefront of the California cooking movement, with its use of fresh, lighter ingredients, an adventuresome spirit, and extraordinary creativity. The growing influence of Pacific Rim flavors and techniques is reflected everywhere, from the proliferation of Japanese sushi bars to the use of Asian spices in the most upscale French restaurants.

79
Restaurants

INDEX BY TYPE

PRICE CATEGORY
- less than $15
- $15–30
- $30–45
- $45–60
- $60 and over

In the area

- ➡ **Where to stay:** ➡ 16
- ➡ **After dark:** ➡ 74
- ➡ **What to see:** ➡ 86 ➡ 88 ➡ 90
- ➡ **Where to shop:** ➡ 128

Where to eat

Ciudad (1)

445 S. Figueroa Street, Los Angeles, CA 90071 ☎ 213/486-5171

(Fifth St.) 🅿 🍴 *Central American* ●●● 🗂 ▭ 🕘 *Mon.–Fri. 11.30am–3.30pm, 5–10.30pm; Sat., Sun. 6.30–10.30pm* ✖ 🎐 *Border Grill* ➡ 58

Mary Sue Milliken and Susan Feniger, of the Border Grill and television's 'Too Hot Tamales,' are now introducing lesser-known delicacies from Central and South America with a dazzling dessert menu and exotic specialty drinks. The wine list is filled with Spanish and Chilean wines.

Cafe Pinot (2)

700 W. Fifth Street, Los Angeles, CA 90071 ☎ 213/239-6500

(Flower St.) 🅿 🍴 *California French* ●●●● 🗂 ▭ 🕘 *Mon.–Fri. 11.30am–2.30pm, 5–9.30pm; Fri. 11.30am–2.30pm, 5-10.30pm; Sat. 5–10.30pm; Sun. 5–9pm* 🍸 ⬆ *on the terrace* ✖

This restaurant is famous for its spectacular decor, its vast picture windows, its enchanting patio adjacent to the historic Central Library, and the Californian accent given to French bistro cuisine. Located no more than a stone's throw from Bunker Hill, the restaurant is almost exclusively frequented in the evenings by people dining out before the show. A complimentary shuttle service is provided to take you to the L.A. Music Center.

Water Grill (3)

544 S. Grand Avenue, Los Angeles, CA 90071 ☎ 213/891-0900

(5th and 6th Sts) 🅿 🍴 *Seafood* ●●●● 🍴 ▭ 🕘 *Mon., Tue. 11.30am–4pm, 5–9pm; Wed.–Fri. 11.30am–4pm, 5–10pm; Sat. 5–10pm; Sun. 4.30–9pm; closed Christmas Day* 🍸

Handsome and elegant, traditional and clubby are words that best describe L.A.'s top seafood house. Located around the corner from the Biltmore and Checker's hotels, this great spot for a power lunch is also a relaxed place for dinner or a quick pre-theater bite at the bar. The raw seafood bar is spectacular, and there's a daily-changing menu of superb cooked dishes. Intelligent service, an excellent wine list and some of the city's best desserts all round out the superlatives for this winning Downtown favorite.

Original Pantry Cafe (4)

877 S. Figueroa Street, Los Angeles, CA 90017 ☎ 213/972-9279

(9th St.) 🅿 *American* ● 🗂 🕘 *open 24hrs daily*

This old-fashioned establishment's main claim to fame is its proprietor, Richard Riordan, mayor of Los Angeles. It has been offering generous proportions of home-cooked and inexpensive food since 1924, seven days a week, 24 hours a day. Famous for its breakfasts of huge omelets, pancakes and French toast heaped with extras.

Not forgetting

■ **City Pier Seafood (5)** 333 S. Spring Street, Los Angeles, CA 90013 ☎ 213/617-2489 ● *This new little snack bar in the Wells Fargo Center offers quality seafood simply prepared, at very affordable prices.*

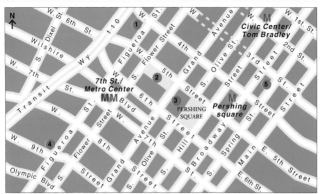

3

By day, Downtown restaurants cater to businessmen, lawyers, politicians, and other white collar workers. At night, it's mostly tourists and theatergoers who patronize the Downtown area's decidedly upscale bastions of fine dining.

Where to eat

Empress Pavilion (6)
988 N. Hill Street, Los Angeles, CA 90012 ☎ 213/617-9898

(Bambou Plaza, Bernard St.) 🅿 🔳 *Chinese* ●● ▭ ◷ *Mon.–Fri. 9am–10pm;
Sat., Sun. 8am–10pm* 🔳

L.A.'s favorite Dim Sum emporium is this authentic Hong Kong-style
seafood house, which can seat almost 600 people in several large rooms.
Service is efficient and fast, with runners and servers rolling carts of
sizzling and steaming dumplings across the room. There are over 175
regular dishes to choose from: either point to what you want or ask for
such special treats as sauteed prawns with honey-glazed walnuts,
barbecued pork in a sweet red glaze or winter melon stuffed with egg,
pork, and shredded dried scallops.

Mandarin Deli (7)
727 N. Broadway, Los Angeles, CA 90012 ☎ 213/623-6054

(between Alpine and Ord Sts) 🅿 *Chinese* ● ▭ ◷ *daily 11am–8pm; closed on
the last Thursday of the month* 🔳 *356 E. Second St., Little Tokyo, Los Angeles*
☎ *213/617–0231*

There is not much atmosphere at this Chinatown noodle and dumpling
shop but the bargain basement prices make up for the lack of ambience.
Choose from the delectable pan-fried dumplings, scallion pancakes or the
huge array of thick, hand-cut noodles, as well as the savory noodle soups
and cold noodle dishes.

Ocean Seafood (8)
750 N. Hill, Los Angeles, CA 90012 ☎ 213/687-3088

(between Alpine and Ord Sts) 🔳 *Chinese* ●● ▭ ▭ ◷ *daily 8am–8pm* 🔳

This vast Hong Kong-style, Cantonese seafood palace at the heart of old
Chinatown serves such specialties as baked crab with ginger, deep-fried,
crispy chicken and dim sum seven days a week, but you should go at the
weekend to really appreciate its frenzied atmosphere when cart after
cart tear along laden with steamed, fried, boiled dumplings and other
delicacies.

Philippe the Original (9)
1001 N. Alameda Street, Los Angeles, CA 90012 ☎ 213/628-3781

(Ord St.) 🅿 *American* ● ◷ *daily 6am–10pm*

Since 1908, hordes of hungry diners have lined up for beef, pork and
lamb French dip sandwiches (they were supposedly invented here) at
this funky landmark with long communal tables and sawdust on the
floors. This nostalgic bit of 'old L.A.' at the edge of Chinatown is a
favorite lunch spot for downtown politicos, lawyers and businessmen;
and it's a convenient stop before a Dodger game at Chavez Ravine.

Not forgetting

■ **Yang Chow (10)** 819 N. Broadway, Los Angeles, CA 90012 ☎ 213/625-0811
●● *If you believe its fans, this is the best restaurant in Chinatown – or in L.A.
The slippery shrimps, the lamb with shallots and the kung pao chicken are some
of the favorites. There is another branch in Pasadena.*

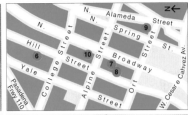

Much of the Asian population is now centered in the San Gabriel Valley and Orange County, but you can still find excellent restaurants and food shops in the historic Chinatown section, north of L.A.'s Civic Center. A number of Vietnamese pho (noodle soup) shops, restaurants and markets have begun to pop up in the neighborhood due to expanding Vietnamese immigration.

➡ Where to eat

Yujean Kang's (11)
67 N. Raymond Avenue, Pasadena, CA 91103 ☎ 626/585-0855

(between Union and Holly Sts) 🔲 *Chinese* ●●●● ▣ 🕐 *Sun.–Fri. 11.30am–2.30pm, 5–9.30pm; Sat. 11.30am–2.30pm, 5–10.30pm*

Yujean Kang, chef and owner, adds a very personal touch to the highly sophisticated cuisine. The cellar, made up of lovingly selected rare and vintage wines from California, France and Germany, reflects Yujean's passion for the grape. The service ·is excellent and the simple, elegant decor is enlivened by subtle Chinese motifs and muted red walls.

All India Café (12)
39 S. Fair Oaks, Pasadena, CA 91105 ☎ 626/440-0309

(Colorado Blvd) 🅿 🔲 *Indian* ● ▣ 🕐 *Sun.–Thu. 11.30am–10pm; Fri., Sat. 11.30am–11pm* 👥 *12113 Santa Monica Blvd, West Los Angeles ☎ 310/442-5250*

Opened by the former chef of West L.A.'s revered Bombay Cafe ➡ 54, Santokh Singh, this new Eastside version offers a similar menu at lower prices. There is a large selection of tandooris, curries and Indian snacks.

Bistro 45 (13)
45 S. Mentor Avenue, Pasadena, CA 91106 ☎ 626/795-2478

(between Colorado Blvd and Green St.) 🔲 *California French* ●●●● 🗂 📱 ▣ 🕐 *Tue.–Fri. 11.30am–2.30pm, 6–9pm; Sat., Sun. 6–9pm; closed for Thanksgiving and Christmas* 🍷 ⭐

This is excellent California-French cuisine, including game and seafood, served in an elegantly restored Art-Deco building on a quiet street far from the bustle of the Old Town. Robert Simon, the proprietor, is a perfectionist who has compiled an impressive wine list.

Parkway Grill (14)
510 S. Arroyo Parkway, Pasadena, CA 91105 ☎ 626/795-1001

(between California and Del Mar Blvds) 🔲 *Californian* ●●●● 📱 ▣ 🕐 *Mon.–Fri 11.30am–2.30pm, 5.30–10pm; Sat., Sun. 5–10pm* 🍷

This restaurant was the first to introduce casual, Westside-style dining to a conservative Pasadena clientele. Dining is served in a room of massive proportions, with big skylights, a profusion of plants and a superb mahogany bar. Choose a salad from the restaurant's own organic garden, then move on to the house specialty, black bean soup, followed by a mesquite-grilled meat dish and, finally, an old-style, home-cooked bread pudding of cheesecake. The wine list specializes in selections from the Napa Valley and other Northern California products.

Not forgetting

■ **Mi Piace (15)** 25 E. Colorado Blvd, Pasadena, CA 91105 ☎ 626/975-3131 ●● *A festive atmosphere, affordable prices and generous portions make this one of the most popular dining spots in Old Town Pasadena. For dessert, the adjacent Pasadena Bakery, under the same ownership, offers excellent baked goods.* ■ **Buca di Beppo (16)** 80 W. Green St., Pasadena, CA 91105 ☎ 626/792-7272 ●● *Eccentric, provocative, amusing, and offering exceptional value for money, Italian family cuisine is served here with generosity – and a smile – in a bawdy, kitsch and fun-filled 1950s atmosphere.*

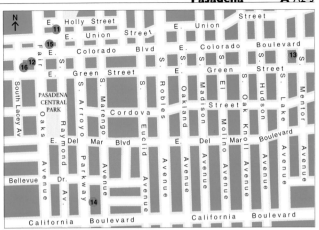

11

11

Most of Pasadena's major restaurants are in the Old Town section, on Colorado Boulevard, and along its side streets, lined by scores of casual, eclectic restaurants. Most are fun, noisy and boisterous; if crowds overwhelm you, seek out some of the quieter, more civilized places on such streets as Raymond or Lake avenues.

mi Piace

13

11

11

Where to ea

Dar Maghreb (17)
7651 Sunset Boulevard, Hollywood, CA 90046 ☎ 323/876-7651

(Stanley Ave) 🎵 **Moroccan** ●●● 🍴 🗂 ▭ ♡ *Mon.–Fri. 6pm–11pm; Sat. 5.30pm–11pm; Sun. 5.30–10.30pm* 🔲 *on the terrace* ✶

Considered the best of the city's albeit few Moroccan restaurants, Dar Maghreb has delighted tourists and locals alike for more than 25 years. Traditional Moroccan menu eaten around low communal tables. Seductive belly dancers enhance this unusual culinary and visual treat.

Pink's Famous Chili Dogs (18)
709 N. La Brea Avenue, Los Angeles, CA 90038 ☎ 323/931-7594

(Melrose Ave) 🅿 **American** ● ♡ *daily 9.30am–2am*

A trip to L.A. is not complete without tasting a famous chili dog from Pink's hot dog stand, an institution that's been family owned since its founding over 60 years ago. There is seating in the back and the crowd is a cross-section of the city's populace – everyone goes to Pink's.

Citrus (19)
6703 Melrose Avenue, Los Angeles, CA 90038 ☎ 323/857-0034

(Citrus Ave) 🎵 **French Californian** ●●●●● ▭ ♡ *Mon.–Fri. noon–2pm, 6.30–9pm; Sat., Sun. 6–9pm; closed at Christmas, New Year, Easter* 🍸

Founding chef and pastry wizard Michel Richard was a culinary trendsetter in the late '80s, creating dishes and a quintessential California style of dining. While the restaurant is still highly regarded, Michel is no longer a major guiding force, spending most of his time at his newer Citronelle in Washington, D.C. Citrus' glass-fronted exhibition kitchen, revolutionary at the time, is still considered a masterpiece and offers diners a theatrical dining experience. Michel's genius as a pastry chef is still evident in the quality of pastries and desserts.

Patina (20)
5955 Melrose Avenue, Los Angeles, CA 90038 ☎ 323/467-1108

(Cole Ave) 🎵 **Franco-Californian** ●●●●● 🗂 🍴 ▭ ♡ *Sun.–Thu. 6–9.30pm; Fri. noon–2pm, 6–9.30pm; Sat. 5.30–10.30pm* 🍸 🔲 *on the terrace* ✶

Sleek and elegant, this renowned gastronomic temple, close to Hollywood's Paramount Studios, is the creation of extraordinary chef Joachim Splichal, who with his wife Christine has spawned a giant empire of successful upscale bistros and cafes (Pinot Bistro, Café Pinot, etc.). Superlatives abound for the stellar food, artistic presentation, serious wine list and very professional service at L.A.'s favorite special occasion restaurant.

Not forgetting

■ **Musso & Frank Grill (21)** 6667 Hollywood Boulevard, Hollywood, CA 90028 ☎ 323/467-7788 ●●● *Enjoy a Martini at the bar, a full all-day breakfast or chops and succulent grilled steaks in this venerable, paneled institution that opened in 1919.* ■ **Miceli's (22)** 1646 N. Las Palmas St., Hollywood, CA 90028 ☎ 323/466-3438 ● *Founded in 1949, this old-fashioned pizza and pasta joint is located in the heart of old Hollywood, walking distance to the recently restored Egyptian Theater.*

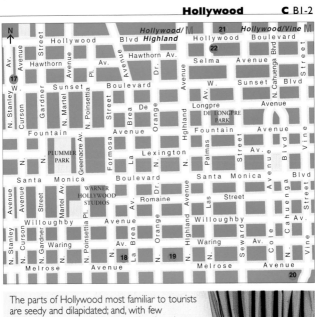

The parts of Hollywood most familiar to tourists are seedy and dilapidated; and, with few exceptions, good eating places are hard to find. Serious eaters would do better heading west to the incorporated city of West Hollywood, one of the Southland's liveliest, most restaurant-intense enclaves.

A climate that is like an almost never-ending summer, lush vegetation, a wide, sandy coast stretching as far as the eye can see and cool, secluded valleys characterize the look of Los Angeles. Restaurants know how to take best advantage of these assets: terraces with views; shady patios and flower-filled gardens are the rule, offering beauty and luxury.

Where to ea

The Restaurant (23)
Bel-Air Hotel, 701 Stone Canyon Rd, Bel-Air, CA 90077 ☎ 310/472-1211

California French ●●●●● 🗋 🍴 ▭ ⊙ *daily 11am–2pm, 6–10pm / Sunday brunch 10am–2pm* 🄿 *on the terrace* 🆈 ✖

The dining room and every nook and cranny of the hotel property are famous for their beauty, elegance and fairy-tale qualities. Dining on the terrace, surrounded by lush gardens and a bower of bougainvilleas, is especially magical and serene, part of the quintessential Los Angeles experience. Under the direction of executive chef Gary Clauson, the food can be spectacular, and service doesn't get much better. Book way in advance, and ask for a seat on the patio.

Gladestone's Four Fish (24)
17300 PCH, Pacific Palisades, CA 90272 ☎ 310/573-0212

(Sunset Blvd) 🅿 🗋 *Seafood* ●●● 🗋 ▭ ⊙ *Mon.–Thu. 11am–11pm; Fri. 11am–midnight; Sat. 7am–midnight; Sun. 7am–11pm* 🄿 *on the terrace* 🆈 ✖ 🍧

This L.A. landmark is a great place to enjoy a spectacular sunset over the sprawling California coastline. Expect large crowds, especially when the weather is good, and be prepared for a long wait for a table. Because the food is overshadowed by the view, consider going for drinks only.

Michael's (25)
1147 Third Street, Santa Monica, CA 90403 ☎ 310/451-0843

(between Wilshire and California Blvds) 🅿 🗋 *American* ●●●●● 🗋 🍴 ▭ ⊙ *Mon.–Sat. 11.30am–2.30pm, 6–10.30pm* 🄿 *on the terrace* 🆈 ✖

The patio, with its lush garden, is where the choice seating is at this ultra-chic spot; although eating inside allows diners to enjoy the restaurant's contemporary art collection. Michael McCarty, one of the groundbreaking restaurateurs of early California cuisine, opened his restaurant over 20 years ago. The food is better than ever, with Korean-born chef Sang Yoon in the kitchen, and wine service is knowledgeable under David Rosoff.

The Lobster (26)
1602 Ocean Avenue, Santa Monica, CA 90401 ☎ 310/458-9294

(Colorado Blvd) 🗋 *Seafood and American* ●●●● 🗋 ▭ ⊙ *Sun.–Thu. 11.30am–3pm, 5–10pm; Fri., Sat. 11.30am–11pm* 🄿 🆈 ✖ 🍧

Located at the entrance to the Santa Monica pier ➡108, The Lobster has reopened its doors with a highly sophisticated, contemporary look, and diners can enjoy a panoramic view of the coast. Its seafood menu has been updated – try the lobster cocktail, the steamed mussels, the spicy prawns, the crab cake and for dessert a Banana Betty.

Not forgetting

■ **Le Petit Four (27)** Sunset Plaza, 8654 Sunset Boulevard, West Hollywood, CA 90069 ☎ 310/652-3863 ●● *Located in the 'middle of the action' in the Sunset Plaza area of the Sunset Strip, this busy sidewalk café is one of L.A.'s favorite European meeting places. The bistro-style menu is top notch, as are the pastries, which is not surprising since the café began as a French patisserie.*

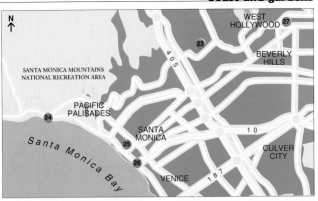

In the area

- **Where to stay:** ➡ 22 ➡ 24
- **After dark:** ➡ 68 ➡ 72 ➡ 74 ➡ 76 ➡ 78 ➡ 82
- **What to see:** ➡ 86 ➡ 100 ➡ 102
- **Where to shop:** ➡ 126 ➡ 138 ➡ 140

Where to ea

Jozu (28)
8360 Melrose Avenue, Los Angeles, CA 90069 ☎ 323/655-5600

(Sweetzer Ave) 🎴 *Pan-Asian* ●●●● 🔲 🔳 🔲 🔲 *Mon.–Thu. 6–10pm;
Fri. 6–11pm; Sat. 5.30–11pm; Sun. 5.30–9.30pm*

In a city known for overnight stardom, this slick, understated creation of restaurateur Andy Nakano quickly rose to the upper echelons of L.A.'s best restaurants in a very short time. Although its original chef has since left, the kitchen continues to turn out inventive, well-executed Pacific Rim fusion dishes, such as sauteed scallops with green curry sauce, saffron and cellophane noodles and crisp sweetbreads with tamarind.

Lucques (29)
8474 Melrose Avenue, Los Angeles, CA 90069 ☎ 323/655-6277

(La Cienaga Blvd) 🎴 *Mediterranean-Californian* ●●●● 🔲 🔲
🕐 *Tue.–Sat. noon–2.30pm, 6–11pm; Sun. noon–2.30pm, 6–10pm* 🔳

This instantly successful hot spot is the domain of talented young chef and co-owner Suzanne Goin. The menu is based on fresh Farmer's Market ingredients and changes every 6–8 weeks. The Sicilian rabbit with escarole, currants and pine nuts on a bed of barley is a knockout, as is the mascarpone polenta with chanterelles, wilted frisee, tomatoes and burrata cheese. This former carriage house on silent film star Harold Lloyd's estate has been transformed into a warm brick and timbered dining room with an enclosed patio in the back. Late-nighters can eat at the bar and order from a scaled-down menu until 1.30am on weekdays.

Matsuhisa (30)
129 N. La Cienaga Boulevard, Beverly Hills, CA 90211 ☎ 310/659-9639

(Wilshire Blvd) 🅿 *Japanese* ●●●●● 🕐 *Mon.–Fri. 11.45am–2.15pm;
5.45–10.15pm; Sat., Sun. 5.45–10.15pm* 🔳 *Ubon 8630 Beverly Blvd
☎ 310/854-1115* ●●

Nobu Matsuhisa, the creator and executive chef, has taken Japanese food to new heights in this unpretentious culinary mecca by adding Peruvian accents to his imaginative dishes. While the sushi is impeccable, the restaurant is best known for its cooked dishes, such as 'squid' pasta with asparagus in garlic butter, black cod in miso sauce, shiitake mushrooms stuffed with sea urchin roe.

Not forgetting
■ **Zen Grill (31)** 8432 W. Third St., Los Angeles, CA 90048 ☎ 323/655-9991 ●● *This noisy, frenetic café serves generous portions of dishes from various parts of Asia. The service is quite casual but it's hip, reasonable and a lot of fun.*
■ **L'Orangerie (32)** 903 N. La Cienaga Blvd, West Hollywood, CA 90069 ☎ 310/652-9770 ●●●●● *A grand and romantic restaurant with a classic but creative French cuisine, subtly enlivened by the use of exotic herbs and spices.*
■ **Locanda Veneta (33)** 8638 W. Third St., Los Angeles, CA 90048 ☎ 310/274-1893 ●●● *The chef and proprietor Antonio Tomasso serves his delicious Venetian specialties in a rustic and cozy setting.* ■ **Lawry's Prime Rib (34)** 100 N. La Cienaga Blvd, Beverly Hills, CA 90211 ☎ 310/652-2827 ●●●● *This beloved L.A. landmark, with its large, comfortable booths and rolling silver carts, has served the same basic menu since it opened in 1938: big slabs of prime rib cut to order tableside, Yorkshire pudding and sides of creamed vegetables.*

48

The Beverly Center, a huge shopping mall, is home to numerous first-class restaurants but also to those inevitable fast-food chains. Third Street, which runs along it to the south, boasts an eclectic collection of small cafés and restaurants, while in the legendary Restaurant Row of La Cienaga, the establishments are generally larger and more traditional.

In the area
➤ **Where to stay:** ➥ 24
➤ **After dark:** ➥ 70 ➥ 72
➤ **What to see:** ➥ 86 ➥ 102
➤ **Where to shop:** ➥ 126 ➥ 142

Where to ea

Maple Drive (35)
345 N. Maple Drive, Beverly Hills, CA 90210 ☎ 310/274-9800

(Alden Dr.) 🏢 *American* ●●●● 🍷 ▣ 🕐 *Mon.–Fri. 11.30am–2.45pm, 6–10pm; Sat. 6–10pm* 🍸 ✦

This sophisticated New American is somewhat hidden in an office complex on the outskirts of Beverly Hills, but finding it is well worth the search. At lunchtime, entertainment industry types come to talk 'show biz', but at night, the crowd comes to eat and enjoy the very good jazz. Recommended dishes include the mouthwatering interpretations of meatloaf and chili.

Nate 'n' Al's (36)
414 N. Beverly Drive, Beverly Hills, CA 90210 ☎ 310/274-0101

(Rodeo Dr.) 🅿 *Delicatessen* ● ▣ 🕐 *closed on Jewish holidays*

A legendary, family-owned institution in the heart of Beverly Hills, offering some of the Westside's best Jewish deli fare. Celebrity watchers can often spot some of the old and new; Hollywood elite indulging in huge corned beef sandwiches, blintzes and chicken soup with matzo balls.

Crustacean (37)
9646 Little Santa Monica Blvd, Beverly Hills, CA 90210 ☎ 310/205-8990

(N. Bedford Dr.) 🅿 🏢 *Vietnamese* ●●●● 🍷 🍴 🕐 *Mon.–Thu. 11.30am–2.30pm, 5.30–10pm; Fri. 11.30am–2.30pm, 5–11pm; Sat. 5.30–11pm* 🍸 ✦

Three generations of the An family have captured the grandeur of French Colonial Vietnam in this gorgeous, celebrity-filled restaurant. A tropical bamboo garden, multi-level verandas and a dramatic koi-filled aquarium that weaves an underground, serpentine path through the restaurant are a few of its extraordinary features. Executive chef Helene An skillfully uses herbs and aromatic spices to accentuate such dishes as roast Dungeness crab and grilled tiger prawns with garlic noodles. The handsome bar is a great place to sample Asian tapas.

Spago Beverly Hills (38)
176 N. Canyon Drive, Beverly Hills, CA 90210 ☎ 310/385-0880

(Wilshire Blvd) 🏢 *Californian* ●●●●● 🍷 ▣ 🕐 *Mon.–Fri. 11.30am–2.15pm, 5.30–10.30pm; Sat. noon–2.15pm, 5.30–11.30pm; Sun. 5–10.30pm* 🍽 *on the terrace* ✦ 🍴 *1114 Horn Ave, West Hollywood* ☎ *310/652-3706* ●●●

Spago Beverly Hills is the toughest reservation in town, but this is world-class California cuisine, with stellar desserts and wine selections and a true 'dining as theater' ambiance. Owner/chef Wolfgang Puck is a household word in the U.S. and, unlike many other superstar chefs, he is usually at his restaurant, working the room. The newer Beverly Hills location is more celebrity-studded, but the original West Hollywood spot still does a fine job – and reservations there are easier to obtain.

Not forgetting

■ **Nouveau Cafe Blanc (39)** 9777 Little Santa Monica Blvd, Beverly Hills, CA 90210 ☎ 310/888-0108 ●●● *Owner/chef Tommy Harase cooks some of L.A.'s best French-Japanese food. Dinner menus change seasonally, and lunch is surprisingly reasonable. There are just ten tables, so reserve ahead.*

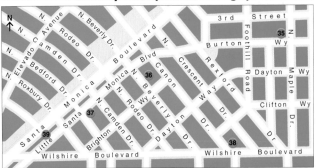

39

38

37

Most visitors to L.A. include a
stop in glamorous Beverly Hills:
to shop on Rodeo Drive, to dine
at its trendy restaurants or to
endeavor to spot a celebrity.
Most upscale Beverly Hills
eateries are located within its
'golden triangle', but many of the
more moderately priced spots
are along Beverly Drive, just
south of Wilshire Boulevard.

Where to ea

Mimosa (40)
8009 Beverly Boulevard, Los Angeles, CA 90048 ☎ 323/655-8895

(N. Edinburgh Ave) 🔊 *French* ●●●● ▢ ◷ *daily 11.30am–2.30pm,
5.30–10.30pm* ▮

With its sunny, yellow walls and cozy ambience, this small, very pretty,
French bistro has a true Provencal feeling. Nice details abound, with crocks
of cornichons and olives on each table and family photographs adorning
the walls. The authentic bistro fare is expertly executed by chef Jean-Pierre
Bosc, and the menu includes several dishes (aligot, hanger steak and veal
daube) not often found in more mundane French bistros.

Authentic Café (41)
7605 Beverly Boulevard, Los Angeles, CA 90036 ☎ 323/939-4626

(N. Curson Ave) 🔊 *Eclectic* ●● ⬚ ▢ ◷ *Mon.–Thu. 11.30am–10pm; Fri.
11.30am–11pm; Sat. 9.30am–11pm; Sun. 9.30am–10pm* ▮ *on the terrace* ✱

This extremely popular restaurant is casual, funky and inexpensive. The
menu ranges from the Mexican *nacho* to Californian pizzas and Chinese
dumplings. The all-day breakfast includes Mexican specialties as well as
American classics: eggs, pancakes and French toast. The portions are
enormous, but expect to wait as you can't make reservations.

Gumbo Pot (42)
**Farmer's Market, 6333 W. Third Street, Los Angeles,
CA 90036 ☎ 323/933-0358**

(Fairfax Ave) 🄿 *Southern United States* ● ▢ ◷ *Mon.–Sat.
10.30am–6.30pm; Sun. 10.30am–5pm* ▮

Probably the best Cajun/Creole food in L.A. is served at this inexpensive
takeout stand. Order at the counter and sit outside eating authentic
muffulatta sandwiches, gumbo, jambalaya and blackened catfish.

Campanile (43)
624 S. La Brea Avenue, Los Angeles, CA 90036 ☎ 323/938-1447

(between 6th and Wilshire Blvd) 🔊 *Californian-Mediterranean* ●●●●● ⬚ ▢
◷ *Mon.–Thu. 11.30am–2.30pm, 6–8pm; Fri. 11.30am–2.30pm, 5.30–11pm;
Sat.9.30am–1.30pm, 5.30–11pm; Sun. 9.30am–1.30pm* ▮ ✱ ▦ *La Brea Bakery*

Campanile is in a beautifully restored palazzo-style building once owned
by Charlie Chaplin. The restaurant is the creation of talented chefs Mark
Peel and his wife Nancy Silverton, who is responsible for the ambrosial
desserts. Its sophisticated yet rustic Mediterranean fare is complemented
by a superb wine list.

Not forgetting

■ **KoKoMo Café (44)** Farmer's Market, 6333 W. Third Street, Los Angeles,
CA 90036 ☎ 323/933-0773 ● *This hip outdoor breakfast and lunch spot at the
L.A. Farmer's Market is an entertainment industry favorite. Hordes of tourists show
up for superb strawberry pancakes, classic turkey hash, burgers and sweet-potato
fries.* ■ **Sofi (45)** 8030 3/4 W. Third Street, Los Angeles, CA 90048 ☎ 323/
651-0346 ●● *This treasure, hidden in an alleyway off Third Street, dishes up some of the
best Greek food this side of Mykonos. Ask for a table on the bougainvillea-decked patio.*

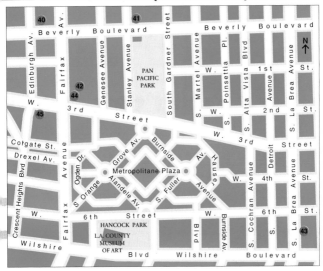

The streets along Beverly Boulevard and Fairfax and La Brea avenues are lined with interesting shops, art galleries and restaurants. The venerable Farmer's Market, established in 1934, with its colorful assortment of outdoor food stands is a great place to have breakfast.

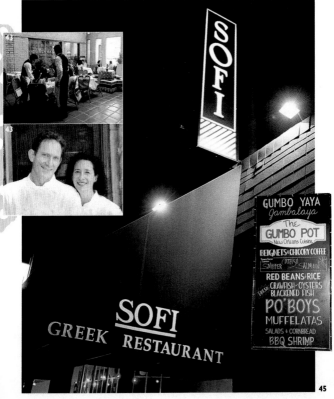

Where to ea

La Cachette (46)

10506 Little Santa Monica Boulevard, West Los Angeles, CA 90025 ☎ 310/470-4992

(between Beverly Glen Blvd and Overland Ave) 🎏 *French* ●●●● 🍴 ▭ ⊙
Mon.–Fri. 11.30am–2.30pm, 6–10.30pm; Sat. 5.30–11pm; Sun. 5.30–9.30pm

At this celebrated restaurant, charismatic chef/owner Jean François Meteigner successfully combines classic French dishes with a light California touch: a perfect choice for refined business or social dining. Try one of Jean François' tantalizing foie gras dishes, the Dungeness crab and lobster bisque, but save room for the award-winning tarte Tatin.

Woodside (47)

11604 San Vincente Boulevard, Brentwood, CA 90049 ☎ 310/571-3800

(Federal Ave) 🅿 *American* ●●●● ▭ ⊙ *Mon.–Thu. 11.30am–2pm, 5.30–10pm; Fri. 11.30am–2pm, 5.30–11pm; Sat. 5.30–11pm; Sun. 5–10pm*

This Westside favorite with its brick walls and gleaming open kitchen is somewhat of a sleeper, but its imaginative, ambrosial food is far better than at most of the trendy restaurants that surround it. Chef Dean Max crafts his menus, taking advantage of seasonal California produce to create imaginative and well-executed dishes. Menu suggestions include fried calamari, a grilled stuffed pork chop, and a variety of desserts.

Il Moro (48)

11400 W. Olympic Blvd, West Los Angeles, CA 90025 ☎ 310/575-3530

(Purdue Ave) 🅿 🎏 *Italian* ●●● ▤ 🍴 ▭ ⊙ *Mon.–Thu. 11.30am–10pm; Fri. 11.30am–10.30pm; Sat. 5.30–10.30pm; Sun. 4.30–9.30pm* ▣ *on the terrace* ✪ ▦

This charming ristorante is tucked into a Westside office building just seconds off the well-traveled #405 freeway. Warm and inviting, it's always packed. The Southern Italian dishes are consistently delicious – ask about the daily specials. Inexpensive to moderately priced Italian and California wines are an added bonus.

Bombay Cafe (49)

12021 W. Pico Blvd, West Los Angeles, CA 90064 ☎ 310/473-3388

(Bundy Ave) 🅿 🎏 *Indian* ●● ▭ ⊙ *Tue.–Thu. 11.30am–3pm, 5–10pm; Fri. 11.30am–3pm, 5–11pm; Sat. 5–11pm; Sun. 5–10pm*

Chef/co-owner Neela Paniz specializes in the street foods and snacks of her native India at this neighborhood cafe. Choose from a list of daily specials or a large assortment of curries, tandoori dishes and frankies or order chats (Indian snacks) with a beer or cocktail. At lunch, order a thali, the traditional metal tray that comes with a selection of dishes.

Not forgetting

■ **Taiko (50)** Brentwood Gardens, 11677 San Vincente Blvd, Los Angeles, CA 90049 ☎ 310/207-7782 ●● *An architecturally stunning oasis of calm serenity near the Getty. Ideal for a quick snack of udon or soba, or you can order sushi, sashimi or one of the specials.* ■ **Apple Pan (51)** 10801 W. Pico Blvd, West Los Angeles, CA 90064 ☎ 310/475-3585 ● *This counter-only shop, opened in 1947, serves superb burgers as well as peerless sandwiches and pies.*

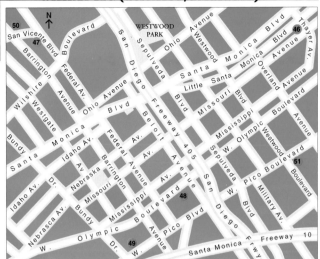

L.A.'s fashionable Westside has many casual outdoor eating places. Choice restaurants are located along San Vincente Boulevard, in Brentwood.

46

49

49

In Los Angeles, you can get a decent meal almost anywhere. However, certain restaurant chains are surprising, with varied menus of consistent quality. The setting can vary from the retro 1950s look to a contemporary décor all in wood, or a minimalist design.

Where to eat

Cheesecake Factory (52)

Pasadena
2 W. Colorado Blvd
☎ 626/584-6000
Beverly Hills
364 N. Beverly Dr.
☎ 310/278-7270
Los Angeles
11647 San
Vincente Blvd
☎ 310/826-7111
Marina del Rey
4142 Via Marina
☎ 310/306-3344
Redondo Beach
605 N. Harbor Dr.
☎ 310/376-0466
🕐 Mon.–Thu.
11am–11pm;
Fri., Sat.
11am–12.30am;
Sun. 10am–11pm
Eclectic ●●
From a single
storefront shop
selling seductively
rich cheesecakes,
The Cheesecake
Factory
metamorphosized
into a chain with

an extensive
menu of
generously
portioned dishes
blending
Californian,
Asian and
Mediterranean
flavors; they are
always crowded,
so be prepared
for a wait.

Daily Grill (53)

Los Angeles
Beverly Center, 100
N. La Cienaga Blvd
☎ 310/451-1655
Brentwood
11677 San
Vincente Blvd
☎ 310/442-0044
Los Angeles International Airport
Tom Bradley Terminal
☎ 310/215-5180
🕐 Tue.–Thu.
11am–3pm,
5–10pm; Fri., Sat.
11am–3pm,

5–11pm; Sun.,
Mon. 5–10pm
American ●●
This casual
spin-off of The
Brentwood
Grill serves no-
nonsense food
in a snappy
bistro setting
reminiscent of
American 'short
order' restaurants
of an earlier era.
It's known for its
Cobb salad, fine
steaks and chops,
as well as
excellent short
ribs, chicken
pot pie and
corned beef hash.
The dessert carte
includes excellent
renditions of such
pure Americana
favorites as apple
pie, rice pudding
and a divine
tapioca pie.

Houston's (54)

Los Angeles
Century City
Center, 10250 S.
Santa Monica Blvd
☎ 310/557-1285
Pasadena
320 S. Arroyo Pkwy
☎ 626/577-6001
Manhattan Beach
1550 Rosecrans Ave
☎ 310/643-7211
🕐 Sun.–Thu.
11.30am–10pm;
Fri., Sat.
11.30am–11.30pm
American ●●
These restaurants
are extremely
popular, with their
dark wood
interiors, their
enormous,
comfortable
booths and their
warm ambience,
enhanced by the
courtesy of the
service. This top-
quality chain
offers food and

service far better than that of many comparable establishments with higher prices. Specializing in large portions of homey American food, including hickory-smoked burgers, prime rib, steaks and terrific barbecued ribs in a tasty, tangy sauce; there are also quite a few pasta and fish options. Don't forget to try the addictive spinach artichoke dip at the bar.

Johnny Rockets (55)

Los Angeles
10250 Santa Monica Blvd
☎ 310/788-9020
Pasadena
One Colorado Blvd

☎ 626/793-6570
Santa Monica
1322 Third St. Promenade
☎ 310/394-6362
Manhattan Beach
Manhattan Market Place,
1550 Rosecrans Ave
☎ 310/536-9464
Long Beach
245 Pine Street
☎ 562/983-1332
🕔 Sun.–Thu. 11am–11pm; Fri., Sat. 11am–midnight
American ●
The nostalgic look of this 1950s style chain is newly manufactured, but the burgers, fries and milkshakes capture the essence of a bygone time; the surprisingly good veggie burgers are definitely a 1990s touch. While prices are higher

than what they were in the 1950s, they're still a bargain by today's standards. Usually located in tourist areas, these 'cool' reminders of an earlier era are popular with anyone wanting to have a good time.

Baja Fresh (56)

Beverly Hills
475 N. Beverly Dr.
☎ 310/858-6690
Brentwood
11690 San Vincente Blvd
☎ 310/826-9166
Santa Monica
720 Wilshire Blvd
☎ 310/393-9313
Marina del Rey
Marina Center,
13424 Maxella Ave
☎ 310/578-2252
Manhattan Beach

Manhattan Village Shopping Center,
3562 Sepulveda Ave
☎ 310/322-5241
Long Beach
5028 E. Second St.,
☎ 562/434-0466
🕔 daily 11am–11pm
Mexican ●
Not much to look at, these brightly lit, almost clinically bare Mexican takeouts serve a wide choice of *burritos* and tacos, based on healthy, fresh products – for example, animal fat is banned. Most customers order takeout as it is not always easy to find a table, especially at the peak lunch period.

In the area

Where to eat

Valentino (57)
3115 Pico Boulevard, Santa Monica, CA 90405 ☎ 310/829-4313

(between 31st and 32nd Sts) 🍴 *Italian* ●●●●● 🔲 ▢ ◷ *Mon.–Thu., Sat. 5.30–10pm; Fri. 11.30am–2.30pm, 5.30–10pm* ▩ ✿

This legendary spot, considered L.A.'s top-rated Italian restaurant for many years, has exquisitely prepared dishes, an extraordinary wine list (considered by many experts to be the best in the U.S.) and exemplary service. Leave the menu to genial owner Piero Selvaggio and the meal will most likely be even more memorable, but be prepared for a hefty bill. The restaurant is elegant, but homey, and is divided into several rooms, with a small patio on the side. Lunch is served on Fridays only.

Border Grill (58)
1445 Fourth Street, Santa Monica, CA 90401 ☎ 310/451-1655

(between Broadway and Santa Monica Blvd) 🅿 🍴 *Central American* ●●● 🔲 ▢ ◷ *Mon. 5–10pm; Tue.–Thu. 11.30am–10pm; Fri., Sat. 11.30am–11pm; Sun. 11.30am–10pm* ▩ ▦ ◨ *Ciudad* ➡ 38

Home to the TV Food Network's 'Too Hot Tamales,' the tempting menu bears little resemblance to those at L.A.'s chain Mexican restaurants. It's fun to sit at the bar or around the large, communal table and enjoy a 'killer' margarita, along with an order of green corn tamales, soft fish tacos or penuchos (black bean filled tortillas with chicken, pickled onions and avocado).

Il Fornario (59)
1551 Ocean Avenue, Santa Monica, CA 90401 ☎ 310/451-7800

(Colorado Ave) 🍴 *Italian* ●●● ▢ ◷ *daily 7am–midnight* ▦ *daily 7am–11pm* ◨ *301 N. Beverly Dr., Beverly Hills* ☎ 310/550-8330

A chain of bakeries in Italy, the Il Fornario restaurants in the U.S. are known for well-prepared, authentic Italian food: salads, pastas, rotisserie chicken and pizzas from the restaurant's wood-burning ovens, as well as superb Italian breads and pastries. The restaurants have a sophisticated, yet rustic, feel; at most locations there is a separate bakery, café and bar.

Not forgetting

■ **Chinois on Main (60)** 2709 Main Street, Santa Monica, CA 90405 ☎ 310/392-9025 ●●●●● *This shining star in the Wolfgang Puck galaxy was a pioneer in merging Asian tastes and techniques with more traditional French and California cuisine. Extremely stylish but small, so dinner reservations should be made far in advance; or try it Wednesday through Friday, when it's opened for lunch.* ■ **El Cholo (61)** 1025 Wilshire Blvd, Santa Monica, CA 90401 ☎ 310/899-1106 ●● *This landmark Mexican restaurant, owned by the same family for five generations, is well known for its traditional dishes in colorful surroundings at inexpensive prices; it's especially famous for its awesome margaritas and green corn tamales.* ■ **Broadway Deli (62)** 1457 Third Street Promenade, Santa Monica, CA 90401 ☎ 310/451-0616 ●● *This cavernous restaurant with its hi-tech interior features not only the traditional choices of hot corned beef sandwiches and matzo ball soup, but also such American favorites as chicken pot pie, Caesar salad, meatloaf and macaroni and cheese. In essence, it's got something for everyone. With a takeout section, bakery, a small market and wine shop, it's also a great place to stop for a coffee or pastries.*

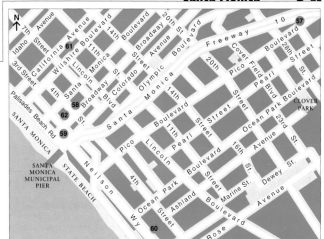

The majority of restaurants in this seaside city are located on the Palisades bluffs along Ocean Avenue, the frenetic Third Street Promenade and on more subdued Main Street. The city is also host to the Wednesday morning Santa Monica Farmer's Market, the biggest and possibly the best outdoor market in the State.

In the area
- ➡ **Where to stay:** ➡ 28 ➡ 30
- ➡ **After dark:** ➡ 68 ➡ 70 ➡ 74 ➡ 80
- ➡ **What to see:** ➡ 86 ➡ 96 ➡ 106 ➡ 108
- ➡ **Where to shop:** ➡ 126 ➡ 144

Where to eat

Joe's (63)
1023 Abbot Kinney Boulevard, Venice, CA 90291 ☎ 310/399-5811

(Broadway) P 🅷 *California French* ●●●● ⬚ ▭ 🕐 *Tue.–Thu. 11.30am–2.30pm, 6–10.30pm; Fri. 11.30am–2.30pm, 6–11pm; Sat. 11am–2.30pm, 6–11pm; Sun. 11am–2.30pm, 6–10.30pm* 🍸 ✳

Everyone loves chef Joe Miller and his very special California food. The restaurant's storefront setting reflects the casual, Bohemian feeling of the Venice area, but service is efficient and the plates are carefully presented. Dinner prices are a relative bargain given the quality of food, and the 3-course lunch is one of the best deals in town. Reservations advised.

Aunt Kizzy's Back Porch (64)
 Villa Marina Shopping Center, 4325 Glencoe Avenue, Marina del Rey, CA 90292 ☎ 310/578-1005

(Mindanao Way) P *Southern United States* ● ⬚ 🕐 *Mon.–Thu. 11am–10pm; Fri., Sat. 11am–11pm; Sun. 11am–3pm*

This regional Southern restaurant serves huge portions of soul food in a very casual setting. Fried catfish and fried chicken, smothered pork chops and barbecued beef ribs, along with sides of black-eyed peas, collard greens, red beans and rice and good old-fashioned cornbread are specialties. At $11.95, the Sunday brunch is a great bargain, but be prepared for cafeteria-style dining, as table service is provided for dinner only.

James' Beach (65)
60 N. Venice Boulevard, Venice, CA 90291 ☎ 310/823-5396

(Pacific Ave) P 🅷 *American* ●●● ⬚ ▭ 🕐 *Mon., Tue. 6–10.30pm; Wed. 11.30am–3pm, 6–10.30pm; Thu., Fri. 11.30am–3pm, 6–1am; Sat. 10am–3pm, 6pm–1am; Sun.10am–3pm* 🌮 *on the terrace* 🍸 ✳

Located half a block from the colorful Venice Boardwalk ➡ 106, it's a favorite gathering spot of the Venice art crowd. Executive chef Shari Lynn Robbins consistently cooks a straightforward, simple menu of American classics (a perfect club sandwich, great fried chicken, and calves' liver). Sunday brunch is an institution here.

Cafe del Rey (66)
4451 Admiralty Way, Marina del Rey, CA 90292 ☎ 310/823-6395

(Bali Way) 🅷 *Pan-Asian* ●●●● 🍴 ▭ 🕐 *Mon.–Thu. 11.30am–2.30pm, 5.30–10pm; Fri., Sat. 11.30am–2.30pm, 5.30–10.30pm; Sun. 10.30am–2.30pm, 5–9.30pm* 🍸 ✳ 🍶

This Pacific Rim favorite delivers great food and service and an exceptional wine list, and it can all be enjoyed with a great marina view.

Not forgetting

■ **C & O Trattoria (67)** 31 Washington Blvd, Marina del Rey, CA 90292 ☎ 310/823-9491 ● *This busy beachside spot is well known for its huge portions of extremely reasonable pasta dishes, and heavenly hot garlic rolls; also a nightly singalong. Go early for dinner or reserving ahead.* ■ **26 Beach Cafe (68)** 26 Washington St., Marina del Rey, CA 90292 ☎ 310/821-8129 ● *Come as you are to this funky patio restaurant by the beach, great for terrific, inexpensive burgers – also made with turkey or veggies – salads and pasta dishes.*

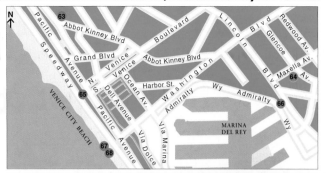

63

Artsy and diversely populated Venice, located north of the small boat harbor of Marina del Rey, far outshines its more elegant neighbor with the number and quality of its restaurants, many of which are located along the stretch of Abbot Kinney Boulevard between Main St. and Venice Blvd.

63

1023

67

26 Beach Café

"mystical touch of elegance that tickles the epicurean"

In the area

- **Where to stay:** ➥ 32
- **After dark:** ➥ 80
- **What to see:** ➥ 86 ➥ 106
- **Where to shop:** ➥ 126 ➥ 144

➡ Where to ea

P.F. Chang's China Bistro (69)
2041 Rosecrans Avenue, El Segundo, CA 90245 ☎ 310/607-9062

(Nash St.) 🅿 🍴 *Chinese* ●● 🔲 🕐 *Sun.–Thu. 11am–11pm; Fri., Sat. 11am–midnight* 🍷 🌟 ♿ *121 N. La Cienaga, Los Angeles ☎ 310/854-6467*

The regional cuisines of Canton, Shanghai, Szechuan, Hunan and Mongolia have been blended with the casual sensibility of California-style dining to produce this successful Chinese mini-chain. An open kitchen, unusual for a Chinese restaurant, and an upscale, modern design with dark wooden floors and hand-painted murals add drama to the room. Food is served MSG-free, and over 40 wines are available by the glass.

Kincaid's Fish, Chop & Steak House (70)
500 The Pier, Redondo Beach, CA 90277 ☎ 310/318-6080

(Torrance Blvd) 🅿 *American and Seafood* ●●● 🔲 🕐 *Mon.–Thu. 11.30am– 10pm; Fri., Sat. 11.30am–11pm; Sun. 10am–8pm* 🔒 *on the terrace* 🍷 🌟 ⛵ 🏢

This imposing new steak and seafood house, located on the Redondo Beach Pier, has been mobbed ever since it opened. The dramatic interior is finished in dark, rich woods, and the soaring walls of glass make good use of the superb seaside location. The menu is an eclectic array of seafood dishes, as well as classic steaks and chops. There can be a lengthy wait for a table, which is made more bearable by the extensive menu of ice-cold margaritas and martinis served in the large, comfortable bar.

Chez Melange (71)
Palos Verdes Inn, 1716 Pacific Coast Highway, Redondo Beach, CA 90277 ☎ 310/540-1222

(Palos Verdes Blvd) 🅿 *Eclectic* ●●● 💳 🔲 🕐 *daily 11am–2.30pm, 5–10pm* 🍷

Known for its eclectic California fare, this popular South Bay pioneer has a menu with choices that range from Pacific Rim tostadas to an award-winning Cajun meatloaf and Asian-style grilled duck. Don't be discouraged by the fact that it's housed in a motel coffee shop, but do note that it has a vibrant bar scene with delicious martinis and a great wine list.

Gina Lee's Bistro (72)
211 Palos Verdes Boulevard, Redondo Beach, CA 90210 ☎ 310/274-9800

(between Catalina Ave and PCH) 🅿 *Eclectic* ●●● 💳 🔲 🕐 *Tue.–Sun. 5–10pm*

This bustling bistro, located in a strip mall not far from the South Bay beaches, has become a local favorite because of its creative, frequently changing menu and its hands-on owners, Gina Lee and her husband Scott, who does the cooking. Fans say the menu, which specializes in seafood with a strong Asian focus, keeps getting better and better. Fresh herbs on each table add a personal touch, and service is friendly.

Not forgetting
■ **Martha's 22nd Street (73)** 25 22nd Street, Hermosa Beach, CA 90254 ☎ 310/376-7786 ● *Open for breakfast and lunch, this basic beach hangout with decent enough food is half a block from the Hermosa Beach boardwalk; go early if you don't want to wait.*

Miles of pristine white sand hug the ocean along the crowded seaside communities of Hermosa, Redondo and Manhattan beaches. It is only recently that the quality of the area's restaurants has begun to keep pace with the influx of newly moneyed young newcomers.

70

73

70

70

Where to ea

King's Fish House / King Crab Lounge (74)
100 W. Broadway, Long Beach, CA 90802 ☎ 562/432-7463

(Pine Ave) 🅿 *Seafood* ●●● ▢ 🕐 *Sun., Mon. 11.15am–9pm; Tue.–Thu. 11.15am–10pm; Fri., Sat. 11.15am–11pm* 🍸 ✦

Actually two restaurants under one roof, the Fish House offers white tablecloth dining in a clubby setting, while the King Crab Lounge is zany and casual, with a patio that overlooks one of Long Beach's main tourist streets. Less formal and expensive than its Downtown sibling, the Water Grill, King's has the same great quality seafood and a large menu that includes several spicy New Orleans-style shrimp dishes.

L'Opera (75)
101 Pine Avenue, Long Beach, CA 90802 ☎ 562/491-0066

(1st St.) 🅿 *Italian* ●●● 🍴 ▢ 🕐 *Mon.–Thu. 11.30am–11pm; Fri. 11.30am–midnight; Sat. 5pm–midnight; Sun. 5–10pm* 🍸

Located in a former bank, L'Opera has long been considered the best Italian restaurant in Long Beach, and perhaps in L.A. It serves exceptional food in a spectacular setting. The wine list has even been awarded prizes; numerous vintage wines are aging in the old bank vaults.

Frenchy's Bistro (76)
4137 E. Anaheim Street, Long Beach, CA 90804 ☎ 562/494-8787

(between Termino and Ximeno Aves) 🅿 *French* ●●● ▢ 🕐 *Tue.–Thu. 11.30am–2.30pm, 5.30–9.30pm; Fri. 11.30am–2.30pm, 5.30–10pm; Sat. 5.30–10pm* 🍸

This friendly sleeper is one of Long Beach's best-kept secrets. It's got a warm, neighborhood feel, and the personal service provided by its caring owners and staff makes every customer feel welcome. The Provençal-inspired menu is filled with such tempting-sounding dishes as venison chops on soft polenta with a balsamic/blackcurrant reduction and pistachio crusted salmon on cod brandade with tomato broth.

Belmont Brewing (77)
Belmont Pier, 25 39th Place, Long Beach, CA 90803 ☎ 562/433-3891

(Ocean Blvd) 🅿 *Eclectic American* ●● 🍴 ▢ 🕐 *Mon.–Fri. 11.30am–10pm; Sat. 10am–10pm; Sun. 9am–10pm* 🍴 *on the terrace* 🍸 ✦ 🍹

This laid-back brewpub at the foot of the Belmont Pier has a spectacular view of the Southern California coast. It's a great place to watch the boardwalk, but if you're here to eat, there's everything from salads, sandwiches, pizza, pasta and substantial main dishes to seared scallops with cilantro pesto and baby back ribs with garlic mashed potatoes.

Not forgetting

■ **Sir Winston's (78)** Queen Mary, 1126 Queen's Highway, Long Beach, CA 90802 ☎ 562/435-3511 ●●●● *The menu is somewhat dated but the classic continental food is better than can be expected at this popular Long Beach tourist attraction.* ■ **Shenandoah Café (79)** 4722 E. Second Street, Long Beach, CA 90803 ☎ 562/434-3469 ●● *This charming country restaurant featuring regional American dishes offers a real meal deal, since entrees come with house fritters and soup or salad.*

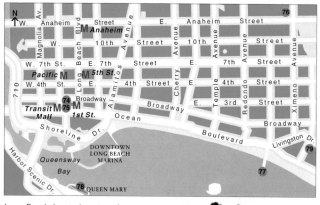

N↑
W. Anaheim Av.
W. Anaheim Street
E. Anaheim Street
W. 10th Street
E. 10th Street
W. 7th St.
E. 7th Street
E. 7th Street
Pacific M
M 5th St.
W. 4th St.
E. 4th Street
E. 4th Street
74
Broadway
Broadway
E. 3rd Street
Transit M
75 M 1st St.
Ocean
Broadway
Shoreline Dr.
Ocean
Boulevard
Livingston Dr.
79
Harbor Scenic Dr.
DOWNTOWN LONG BEACH MARINA
Queensway Bay
77
78 QUEEN MARY

Magnolia Blvd
W. Beach Blvd
Long
Alamitos Avenue
Cherry Avenue
Temple Avenue
Redondo Avenue
Ximeno Avenue
76
710

Long Beach, located next to the busiest trade port in the nation, has gone through a long redevelopment and now boasts such major tourist draws as the *Queen Mary* ➤ 110, the Convention and Entertainment Center and the Aquarium of the Pacific ➤ 110. New restaurants are slowly emerging to meet the needs of tourists.

KINGS fish house

78

65

Opening hours

Most establishments close at 2am when they stop serving alcohol, a measure intended to prevent drunk driving. Others stay open later, especially on Fridays and Saturdays, and alcohol is on sale again from 6am. Ask the staff for details.

After dark

No smoking

There is no special dispensation under Californian law for entertainment venues. You can only smoke on patios, terraces or quite simply in the street!

Entrance charges

Cover (admission) charge
entrance charge
Minimum charge
minimum drinks order
Music charge
supplement for watching a show

Events listings

All local festivities are listed in the *L.A. Weekly* and *New Times* (free papers distributed on Thursdays in most movie theaters, clubs, coffee shops and stores) as well as in the 'Calendar' section of Sunday's *Los Angeles Times*. Get hold of the leaflets advertising local events in independent record stores (on Melrose Avenue).

Age limit

Entry into bars and clubs in Los Angeles is prohibited to those under the age of 21. Make sure you carry photo I.D. Teenagers have their own venues that are listed in the small ads section of local papers or in stores frequented by young people.

63
Nights out

Festivals

The cultural life of Los Angeles, a modern Babylon, reflects the diversity of its population. Hundreds of festivals, often free, take place throughout the year. Before your departure, consult the website: www.culturela.org. When you are there, telephone the L.A. Cultural Affairs Department ☎ 213/485-2433

April Los Angeles Independent Film Festival
June-September Hollywood Bowl Summer Festival
June-October Grand Performances at California Plaza
July-September Santa Monica Pier Twilight Dance Series

In Los Angeles, bars can be casual meeting places or locations with much more style ➡ 70. Most don't offer food, unless they are part of a restaurant. A word of advice: always have photo I.D. with you, as doormen and barmen can ask for evidence of age, even if you are over 30!

After dark

North (1)
8029 Sunset Blvd, West Hollywood, CA 90046 ☎ 323/654-1313

(Laurel Ave) ▣ 🎭 🎰 ▤ 🕓 Mon.–Sat. 6pm–2am; Sun. 7pm–2am ● $6 🍴 Mon.–Sat. 6pm–1am; Sun 7pm–midnight 🅿 on the terrace ⬛

Just off the Sunset Strip, this bar/restaurant has earned high marks among trendsetters with its small yet comfortable split-level floorplan. The main room resembles a ski lodge with its warm wood-paneled interior. Try the Pearl Necklace Cocktail with Crème de Menthe. Reservations required for dinner Fridays or Saturdays if you wish to sit in a booth.

Formosa Café (2)
7156 Santa Monica Blvd, West Hollywood ☎ 323/850-9050

(Formosa Ave) 🎭 ▤ 🕓 Mon.–Fri. 4pm–2am; Sat., Sun. 6pm–2am ● $5 🍴 🅿 on the terrace ⬛

Formosa Café is opposite one of Hollywood's oldest studios, which is why there are countless photos of stars covering the walls. The original bar and restaurant have the feel of a film noir while the new back patio reflects a modern Chinese-American theme. It is best to arrive early, especially at the weekend.

El Carmen (3)
8138 3rd Street, Los Angeles, CA 90048 ☎ 323/852-1552

(Crescent Heights Blvd) 🎭 ▤ 🕓 Mon.–Fri. 5pm–2am; Sat., Sun. 7pm–2am ● $6 🍴

With the charm of a Mexican border saloon, the renovated El Carmen, which dates to 1927, is actually the brainchild of famed restaurateur Sean McPherson of Bar Marmont and the Good Luck Club. Check out the felt paintings of masked wrestlers that adorn the ceiling as well as the ornate tilework while sipping their excellent margaritas – over 200 different kinds of tequila are on hand. Though it is long on attitude and short on service, this has quickly become one of Hollywood's hipster watering holes.

Not forgetting

■ **Circle Bar (4)** 2926 Main Street, Santa Monica, CA 90405 ☎ 310/450-0508 *This local favorite on Santa Monica's popular Main Street has been renovated under the new ownership of Will Karges of Jones and Rix. Candlelit and cozy, the place is always packed so get there early. It's fun to scope out the crowd – Hollywood meets the beach – as you squeeze your way around the circular bar. DJs spin some nights.* ■ **The Room (5)** 1626 N. Cahuenga Blvd, Hollywood, CA 90028 ☎ 323/462-7196 *Seen in the movie Swingers, this spot is all about the mystery of its entrance which is actually at the back; great DJs play this cozy venue.* ■ **Boardner's (6)** 1652 Cherokee Blvd, Hollywood, CA 90046 ☎ 323/462-9621 *Be sure to pass through this grungy bar to enter its charming interior courtyard; four nights of DJ-supplied music.* ■ **Good Luck Bar (7)** 1514 N. Hillhurst Ave, Hollywood, CA 90027 ☎ 323/666-3524 *This bar with a neo-Asian motif, paper lanterns and large, comfy chairs has a young, hip following.* ■ **Liquid Kitty (8)** 11780 W. Pico Blvd, West Hollywood, CA 90064 ☎ 310/473-3707 *This retro-style, smoky bar specializes in old-fashioned cocktails, the music is great and occasionally live.*

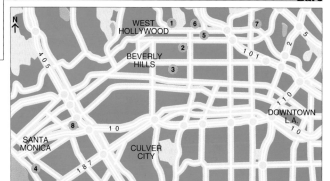

CIRCLE BAR
SANTA MONICA

Traditionally, cocktail lounges are dark, warm and comfortable places where you can go to unwind, listen to music or talk with friends while sipping a Martini with an evocative name (Sex on the Beach, Kamikaze, Manhattan…). Don't be too shy to ask the barman what his specialties are.

After dark

Yamashiro (9)
1999 N. Sycamore Ave, Hollywood, CA 90068 ☎ 323/466-5125

(Franklin Ave) 🚇 ▭ 🕙 *Sun.–Thu. 4.30pm–12.30am; Fri., Sat. 4.30–1.30am* ● *$ 7* 🍴 *Mon.–Thu. 5.30–9.30pm; Fri., Sat. 5.30–10.30pm* 🅿 *on the terrace* ⊠ ⚜

In the hills high above Hollywood this former private house, a copy of a Kyoto palace from 1911, offers a dazzling view of Downtown, Hollywood and the L.A. basin. There is a sushi bar and restaurant, both of which are pricey, but the reason to visit is the cocktail lounge which offers such great rum drinks as a Scorpion or Mai Tai. The best time to visit is at dusk when the lights begin to twinkle over the city.

Lava Lounge (10)
1533 N. La Brea, Hollywood, CA 90028 ☎ 323/876-6612

(Sunset Blvd) 🅿 ▭ 🕙 *daily 9pm–2am* ● *$5; cover charge $4* 🎵

Don't be put off by its unfashionable location in a mini-mall next to a liquor store. Lava Lounge is a palm-thatched Tiki bar that redefines 'kitsch' with a waterfall over real lava rocks, a constellation of stars that twinkle on the ceiling and a small stage featuring live retro-funk, jazz and lounge music. The joint is tiny and can be smoky, so if you don't mind bumping into other hipsters while dancing to live music and the occasional DJ, then Lava is the place to be.

Daddy's (11)
1610 Vine Street, Hollywood, CA 90028 ☎ 323/463-7777

(Selma Ave) 🅿 ▭ 🕙 *Mon.–Sat. 9pm–2am; Fri., Sat. 4.30pm–1.30am* ● *$6*

Near the corner of Hollywood & Vine is Daddy's – formerly Lucky Seven – where the theme is definitely red, with banquettes, padded bar and plush red curtains to match. The attitude is casual and laid back; make a selection from the well-stocked jukebox. This is a good place to hang out with a group of friends or get cozy with your date while sipping a Martini or two. Daddy's is very much a cocktail lounge in the American tradition, but it's dark inside so bring a flashlight.

Not forgetting

■ **Lounge 217 (12)** 217 Broadway, Santa Monica, CA 90401 ☎ 310/394-6336 *A rough concrete wall and a heavy solid wooden door are the distinguishing marks of this otherwise unsignposted bar, renowned for its Martinis. Inside, the diffuse light, simple and elegant décor and unusual atmosphere give it an intimate charm.* ■ **360 (13)** 6290 Sunset Blvd, Hollywood, CA 90028 ☎ 323/871-2995 *Perched on the roof of an apartment block, this restaurant-bar is famous for its view.* ■ **Tiki Ti (14)** 4427 Sunset Blvd, Los Angeles, CA 90027 ☎ 323/669-9381 *It's impossible to have a bad time at this tiny historic Polynesian bar, but call first to be sure it's open.* ■ **Three Clubs (15)** 1123 N. Vine Street, Hollywood, CA 90038 ☎ 323/462-6441 *No sign outside, a dark wood-paneled interior and padded booths are the signature of this classy and highly esteemed venue.* ■ **Trader Vic's (16)** Beverly Hilton, 9876 Wilshire Blvd, Beverly Hills, CA 90210 ☎ 310/274-7777 *This chic but conservative establishment serves world-famous rum-based cocktails and assorted mouthwatering appetizers.*

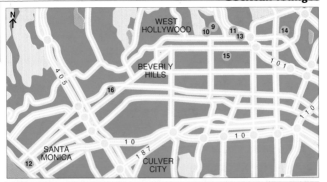

Since the 1930s, the landscape of Sunset Strip has been characterized by its many nightclubs. It is about a mile and a half portion of Sunset Boulevard, from around Crescent Heights to Doheny Drive. Free parking is extremely difficult to find – most of the surrounding areas require permits to park – so be prepared to walk or bite the bullet and pay for valet.

After dark

Whisky A Go Go (17)

8901 Sunset Boulevard, West Hollywood, CA 90069 ☎ 310/652-4202

(San Vincente Blvd) 🅿 ▭ 🕔 *daily 8pm–1am ● $5.50; cover charge $10–12* 🏠

Since 1964 Whisky A Go Go has hosted nearly every major band: The Doors, Jimmy Hendrix, Sonny and Cher, Van Halen and Nirvana. A mostly young crowd flocks to this intimate space where a balcony overlooks a small stage; ideal for seeing your favorite group or rising new talent. Credit cards are accepted except at the door, where the cover charge has to be paid in cash.

Viper Room (18)

8852 Sunset Boulevard, West Hollywood, CA 90069 ☎ 310/358-1881

(Larrabee St.) 🍴 ▭ 🕔 *daily 9pm–2am ● $5; cover charge $10* 🎵

Johnny Depp's Viper Room – the entrance is just off the Strip – plays host to some of L.A.'s hottest nights. Made world-famous by the tragic demise of talented actor River Phoenix on its doorstep, the club is everything that's good and bad about Hollywood after dark. It's small, smoky and hard to get in, but plays host to an array of great nights from House/Progressive DJs to unannounced special gigs by famous bands. Expect to bump into the odd celebrity, especially if you find yourself in the secretive VIP room.

House of Blues (19)

8430 Sunset Boulevard, West Hollywood, CA 90069 ☎ 323/848-5100

(La Cienaga Blvd) 🦜 ▭ 🕔 *daily 8pm–1.30am ● $5; cover charge $18–25* 🏠 *daily 11.30am–midnight* 🅿 *on the terrace* 🎵 🎫 ★

World-class bands on tour often perform their local dates at the Los Angeles venue of this music chain. Looking and feeling somewhat like a Disneyland version of a backwoods blues club – complete with a gift shop – this is a place to hear great music. Expect to stand unless you've made prior dinner reservations; the menu includes Cajun and other Southern specialties. The club also offers a Sunday Gospel Brunch. Be sure to check out the 'native' art hanging on the walls, the symbols of world religions above, and designer Jon Bok's folksy bar.

Not forgetting

■ **Key Club (20)** 9039 Sunset Blvd, West Hollywood, CA 90069 ☎ 310/786-1712 *Deluxe, two-level nightclub with an audience that ranges from flashy to funky, depending upon the show.* ■ **The Roxy Theater (21)** 9009 Sunset Blvd, West Hollywood, CA 90069 ☎ 310/276-2222 *Both famous and promising new bands have graced the stage for industry insiders at this historic rock 'n' roll venue.* ■ **The Sky Bar (22)** Mondrian, 8440 Sunset Blvd, West Hollywood, CA 90069 ☎ 323/650-8999 *An elegant bar located at the top of the Mondrian hotel* ➡ *22, with a superb view over the city. Strict selection at the door.* ■ **Coffee House (23)** 8226 Sunset Blvd, West Hollywood, CA 90046 ☎ 323/848-7007 *Created by promoter extraordinaire Brent Bolthouse, this 24-hour restaurant/coffee shop has a comfy chateau-like ambience.* ■ **Bar Marmont (24)** Chateau Marmont, 8171 Sunset Blvd, West Hollywood, CA 90046 ☎ 323/650-0575 *Stylish nightspot with a Franco-Asian flavor. Hip, upscale place to mingle with Hollywood folk.*

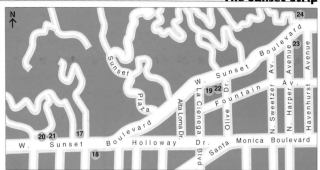

19

19

Los Angeles was once home to a great number of fabulous movie palaces connected to the studios. Many of these architectural gems have been lost or transformed, particularly in Downtown L.A., into retail spaces. A few of the most famous in Hollywood have been saved and are great places to see a movie.

After dark

Egyptian Theater (25)
6712 Hollywood Blvd, Hollywood, CA 90028 ☎ 323/466-3456

(Las Palmas Blvd) 🅿 ▭ 🕐 *variable* ● *$7–15* ✖ 🍽

Sid Grauman built the Egyptian Theater in 1922, and it has hosted countless Hollywood premieres. Today it is the home of the American Cinematheque which has lovingly restored it for their screenings and retrospectives and added state-of-the-art projection and sound. Playing Tuesday through Sunday for visitors is *Forever Hollywood*, an hour-long film that pays homage to Los Angeles and its studios. As the theater is often rented out for special screenings, telephone in advance to find out opening times and prices.

Silent Movie Theatre (26)
611 N. Fairfax Avenue, Los Angeles, CA 90036 ☎ 323/655-2520

(Melrose Ave) 🕐 *Tue.–Fri. 8pm; Sat. 1pm, 8pm; 10.15pm; Sun. 1pm, 8pm* ● *$8; concessions $6* 🅿

One day in 1997, Charlie Lustman, a songwriter, noticed this desolate building, closed since the murder of its proprietor. Upon purchasing it, he discovered a priceless treasure-trove under the stage: over 3,000 silent films. First opened in 1942 by collectors John and Dorothy Hampton, the Silent Movie Theatre has now been reborn. It is the only American movie theater devoted to silent film. Screenings are accompanied by the organ or piano.

Highways Performance Space (27)
1651 18th Street, Santa Monica, CA 90404 ☎ 310/453-1755

(Pico Blvd) 🅿 🕐 *Fri., Sat. 8.30pm; Sun. 5pm* ● *$12–15*

Since May of 1989, this space has presented some of the most innovative performance art, dance and spoken words in Los Angeles. Especially known for its workshops and for featuring the work of gay, lesbian and other minority artists in its 99-seat theater.

Not forgetting

■ **Mann's Chinese Theater (28)** 16925 Hollywood Blvd, Hollywood, CA 90028 ☎ 323/464-8111 *This famous movie palace – site of hundreds of world premieres – is still the place for big films to open; the courtyard has hand and footprints of the stars ➡ 98.* ■ **Odyssey Theater (29)** 2055 S. Sepulveda Blvd, West Los Angeles, CA 90025 ☎ 310/477-2055 *See the stars of tomorrow, in a sprinkling of world premieres from classics to cutting-edge political thrillers, on the three stages of this theater.* ■ **El Capitan (30)** 6838 Hollywood Blvd, Hollywood, CA 90028 ☎ 323/467-7674 *This remodeled movie palace is home to Disney movies and related live stage shows that are even fun for adults.* ■ **Pacific's Cinerama Dome (31)** 6360 Sunset Blvd, Hollywood, CA 90028 ☎ 323/466-3401 *Locals all have fond memories of favorite movies viewed in this architectural landmark, a white geodesic dome.* ■ **The Actors' Gang Theater (32)** 6209 Santa Monica Blvd, Hollywood, CA 90038 ☎ 323/465-0566 *This avant-garde acting troupe, started in part by Tim Robbins, performs consistently striking original work at this theater.* ■ **Mark Taper Forum & Ahmanson Theater (33)** 135 N. Grand Avenue, Los Angeles, CA 90012 ☎ 213/628-2772 *Perhaps the two most widely known and respected theaters in town.*

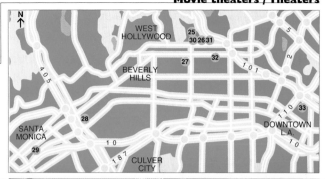

Home of stand-up comedy, Los Angeles welcomes comics from all over the country who hope to get themselves noticed by the movie or television industries. Cabarets put on lounge music that can range from 1950s-60s retro to the most contemporary sounds.

After dark

Dresden Room (34)
1760 N. Vermont Avenue, Hollywood, CA 90027 ☎ 323/665-4294

(Prospect Ave) **P 🎵 ▬ 🕐** *Mon.–Sat. 11.30am–3.30am; Sun. 4–11pm* ● $ 4–7 ▦

This cocktail lounge and restaurant, which over the years has gone in and out of style, has always been consistent in one respect: the singing duo of Marty and Elayne, a lounge act that must be seen to be believed. Their rendition of new songs and old songs is highly entertaining and eccentric. Tuesday is open mike night when you can laugh or groan to lounge tunes being tortured by guest singers.

The Groundlings (35)
7307 Melrose Avenue, Los Angeles, CA 90046 ☎ 323/934-9700

(Fuller Ave) **🎵 ▬ 🕐 shows** *Thu. 8pm; Fri. 8pm, 10pm; Sat. 8pm, 10pm; Sun. 7.30pm; closed Thanksgiving, Christmas* ● $12–18.50 ◼ ♦

The home of sketch comedy and improv features Los Angeles' most celebrated comedy group. Past alumni include Pee Wee Herman, Jon Lovitz and Lisa Kudrow. There is also a school for professional comedic actors as well as those just looking to have a good laugh. Shows vary each evening and reservations are required.

Luna Park (36)
665 N. Roberston, West Hollywood, CA 90069 ☎ 310/652-0611

(Santa Monica Blvd) **🎵** $4 **🍴 🕐** *daily 6pm–2am* ● $4–7; **cover charge** $6 ▦ *Sun., Tue.–Thu. 6.30–11pm; Fri., Sat. 6.30pm–midnight* **🎵** *on the terrace* 🎵 ◼

Jean-Pierre Boccara has created perhaps the best all-around nightclub in Los Angeles. Known for its good food, enjoyable ambience, multi-cultural crowd and eclectic entertainment, it features an impressive range of music from world beat to jazz. There are two stages and three bars, plus a restaurant area and pleasant spacious patio for smoking. On Sunday nights, Beth Lapides hosts Un-Cabaret, acclaimed for presenting unconventional standup comedy.

Not forgetting

■ **Les Deux Cafés (37)** 1638 N. Las Palmas, Hollywood, CA 90028 ☎ 323/465-0509 *This most fashionable of club-restaurants is slap-bang in the middle of a parking lot! Stars of the film and fashion industries go wild about this 1904 building, with its maze of rooms and patios. If you want to blend in with the décor, wear black.* ■ **The Laugh Factory (38)** 8001 Sunset Blvd, West Hollywood, CA 90069 ☎ 323/656-1336 *As its name implies, it's the ideal place for those who enjoy marathon laughter sessions.* ■ **Comedy Store (39)** 8433 W. Sunset Blvd, West Hollywood, CA 90069 ☎ 323/656-6225 *This well-known club on the Sunset Strip is where many comics are discovered.* ■ **The L.A. Improv (40)** 8162 Melrose Ave, Hollywood, CA 90046 ☎ 323/651-2583 *Robin Williams, Jay Leno and Jerry Seinfeld made their debut on the boards of this offshoot of the famous New York club. There's no problem dining at Hell's Kitchen, but it is strongly recommended that you make a reservation for the show.* ■ **Largo (41)** 432 N. Fairfax Ave, Los Angeles, CA 90036 ☎ 323/852-1073 *You can hear a variety of music at this relaxed, elegant club.*

All forms of live music co-exist in Los Angeles: swing, folk, rock, jazz, salsa, pop, even country. Many of the best names in music live and perform here, as the town is home to the biggest record companies. And artists on tour make it a point of honor to perform in the City of Angels.

After dark

Dragonfly (42)
6510 Santa Monica Blvd, Hollywood, CA 90038 ☎ 323/466-6111

(Wilcox Ave) 🚇 ▢ 🕐 *daily 9pm–2am* ● *$4 ; cover charge $5–10* 🅿️ *on the terrace* 🎵 ⭐

This club features some of the best in cutting-edge alternative rock with artists from bands such as Stone Temple Pilots, Rage Against the Machine, Alanis Morissette and Ice T. A large stage and dance floor is surrounded by four bars and an outdoor patio. DJs spin a variety of funk, hip-hop, house and disco. Dragonfly is a casual nightclub where you can rub elbows with Hollywood's elite.

Vynyl (43)
1650 N. Schrader Blvd, Hollywood, CA 90028 ☎ 323/465-7449

(Hollywood Blvd) 🅿️ 🚇 ▢ 🕐 *variable* ● *$5–6; cover charge $10–25* 🎵

Mark Smith, co-owner of the popular North ➡ 68 and Three Clubs ➡ 70, has opened this new live music venue in the heart of Hollywood. At one time a telemarketing center for Frederick's of Hollywood ➡ 132, the space has been remodeled and opened up into a lounge area and a loft-like main room. Popular and critically acclaimed bands such as Sheryl Crow, Basement Jaxx and Afro-Celt Sound System play here for happy dancing youth and industry types alike.

The Conga Room (45)
5364 Wilshire Blvd, Los Angeles, CA 90036 ☎ 323/938-1696

(La Brea Ave) 🅿️ 🚇 🍴 ▢ 🕐 *Thu. 6pm–1am; Fri., Sat. 6pm–1.30am* ● *$7; cover charge $10–25* 🅿️ *on the terrace* 🍴 *La Bocca* 🎵

The Conga Room is one of the finest venues for Latin music and reflects Los Angelinos' growing interest in Afro-Cuban music and the accompanying cuisine. Artists such as Celia Cruz and Pancho Sanchez have graced the stage along with house band Salsa Orchestras. The Conga Room draws a high-intensity crowd in a warm tropical setting so dress up and bring your dance shoes. Salsa dance lessons are available Thursday and Friday evenings.

Not forgetting

■ **Troubadour (46)** 9081 Santa Monica Boulevard, West Hollywood, CA 90068 ☎ 310/276-6168 *If only these walls could tell the story of the Troubadour from the 1960s… This popular venue, established by Doug Weston, is still one of the best places to hear alternative rock, but in more intimate surroundings than a large concert hall.* ■ **The Derby (47)** 4500 Los Feliz Boulevard, Los Feliz, CA 90027 ☎ 323/663-8979 *Vast and elegant, with an enormous circular bar, The Derby is a Hollywood classic where the orchestra plays swing dancing most nights; dance lessons are available.* ■ **The Gig (48)** 7302 Melrose Ave, Hollywood, CA 90046 ☎ 323/936-4440 *Established artists and promising talent perform in this casual club, with two locations.* ■ **Spaceland (48)** 1717 Silver Lake Blvd, Silverlake, CA 90026 ☎ 323/413-4442 *A funky interior and an eclectic audience are characteristic of this establishment in bohemian Silverlake. Admission is often free on Mondays.*

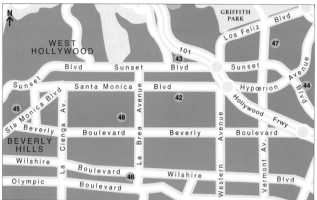

47

43

Los Angeles, although on the decline in recent years, still prides itself on hosting the best in jazz and blues. Some venues are down-at-heel bars in outlying districts, while others are much more elegant with a strict dress code. In all cases, you have to pay a cover charge at the door.

After dark

Catalina Bar & Grill (49)
1640 Cahuenga Boulevard, Hollywood, CA 90028 ☎ 323/466-2210

(Hollywood Blvd) 🅿 ▭ 🕐 daily 9pm–2am ● $4–7; **cover charge** $15–25 🍴 ♫

This elegant, upscale spot has live music six nights a week, featuring some of the finest names in jazz. Along with the Jazz Bakery, this is the place for the top musicians, so expect to pay a bit more for it. Located just off Hollywood Boulevard, the recently renovated dining room has state-of-the-art lighting and sound and it is not uncommon to see a celebrity or two in the crowd.

Harvelle's (50)
1432 Fourth Street, Santa Monica, CA 90401 ☎ 310/395-1676

(Broadway Blvd) 🅿 ▭ 🕐 daily 8pm–2am ● $3.50; **cover charge** Sun.–Thu. $3, Fri., Sat. $5–8 ♫

Cozy, friendly, usually packed, this club specializes in authentic, unpretentious folk blues, an almost incongruous exception in the heart of Santa Monica. You're certain to have a good time and to experience something unique: good blues in an atmosphere totally free of cigarette smoke. Harvelle's, originally a jazz-club-cum-restaurant, has been in existence since 1931 – for Los Angeles this borders on an eternity.

Babe & Ricky's Inn (51)
4339 Leimert Boulevard, Los Angeles, CA 90008 ☎ 323/295-9112

(Leimert Park) 🚇 ▭ 🕐 Mon., Wed.–Sun. 6pm–1.30am ● $3–5; **cover charge** $5 🍴 daily 6–10pm ♫

This blues club, one of the oldest in L.A., exists cheek by jowl with the many restaurants, clubs and cafes of Leimert Park, the epicenter of the black renaissance in Los Angeles. Its walls are plastered with innumerable photos of obscure or legendary artists. Sundays and Mondays are open mike night when talented musicians simply drop in and start jamming. This place is an absolute must.

Not forgetting
■ **B.B. King's Blues Club and Restaurant (52)** 1000 Universal Center Drive, Universal City, CA 91608 ☎ 818/622-5464 *This 350-seat club books top performers like John Lee Hooker or B.B. King himself in Universal's entertainment complex, the City Walk.*
■ **Rocco (53)** 2930 Beverly Glen Circle, Bel-Air, CA 90077 ☎ 310/475-9807 *Enjoy first-class jazz in this elegant restaurant, slightly off the beaten track.*
■ **The Mint (54)** 6010 Pico Boulevard, Los Angeles, CA 90035 ☎ 323/954-9630 *Famous blues and jazz musicians perform in the intimate surroundings of this bar-restaurant every night.*
■ **Jazz Bakery (55)** 3233 Helms Avenue, Culver City, CA 90232 ☎ 310/475-9807 *You can only get drunk on music in this venue for purists (alcohol in the lobby only). The Jazz Bakery is home to the biggest names in jazz.*
■ **5th Street Dick's (56)** 3347 1/2 W. 43rd Place, Los Angeles, CA 90008 ☎ 323/296-3970 *Tiny space in Leimert Park that features established and up-and-coming artists who often push the musical envelope.*

Hollywood, Westside and Sunset Strip are home to the best discotheques in Los Angeles. The music, clientele, clothes and opening times vary daily, depending on the organizer. Phone in advance to find out the program and to check times, or consult the free paper *L.A. Weekly* (every Thursday).

 # After dark

Garden of Eden (57)
7080 Hollywood Blvd, Hollywood, CA 90028 ☎ 323/465-3336

(La Brea Ave) 🅿 🚼 🍴 ⬛ 🕐 *Wed., Thu. 10pm–2am; Fri.–Sun. 9pm–2am*
● *$7–8; cover charge $15* 🎵 *on the terrace* ⭐

This 550-seat Moroccan-style nightclub/lounge has a mix of funk, hip-hop and groove music. Comfortable couches and space heaters make the outdoor patio one of the nicer club smoking areas in town. Arriving early and looking stylish may lessen your wait time to enter. Call first to confirm it's not closed for a private party.

Club 7969 (58)
7969 Santa Monica Blvd, West Hollywood, CA 90069 ☎ 323/654-0280

(Laurel Ave) 🅿 🕐 *daily 9pm–2am* ● *$5; cover charge $10*

Located in the predominantly gay center of West Hollywood, this club features a different clientele each night – gay, straight or transsexual – and often the boundaries overlap. There is even a Topless Revue for women! The best night to go is Saturday for Sin-A-Matic, a fetish club that features scantily clad go-go girls and boys and the notorious 'back room'. But the real star of this venue is the music and the world-class DJs who spin a mix of techno, alternative and industrial sounds.

The Playroom (59)
836 N. Highland Avenue, Hollywood, CA 90028 ☎ 323/460-6630

(Willoughby Ave) 🕐 *Mon., Thu., Fri. 10pm–3am; Sat. 9pm–9am* ● *$5–7; cover charge $10–15*

This purple and black nightspot that was formerly The Probe has a large stage and dance floor, hydraulic go-go cages as well as an upstairs bar and VIP room. Each night varies with music ranging from glam rock to music of the 1980s – Saturday is 'boys' night' – so it's best to call ahead.

Louis XIV (60)
606 N. La Brea Avenue, Hollywood, CA 90036 ☎ 323/934-5102

(Melrose Ave) 🚼 ⬛ 🕐 *daily 6pm–2am* ● *$6* 🍽 🎵 *on the terrace* ⭐

DJs spin from the balcony while the clientele dine and dance in this popular restaurant/nightspot. Enjoy gourmet organic food but expect to wait. Resident DJs, The Bud Brothers, host mixmasters from around the world at their weekly 'Monday Social' while a crowd easily fills the tiny, high-fidelity lounge upstairs. Dinner reservations suggested.

Not forgetting

■ **Voodoo (61)** 4120 Olympic Blvd, Los Angeles, CA 90019 ☎ 323/930-9600 *Just south of Hancock Park, this club has a main room with the feel of an Indiana Jones temple with a voodoo twist; the raised copper dance floor is fenced off with large femur bone-shaped posts. Intimate VIP rooms are upstairs and music ranges from live jam sessions to Latin, house and hip-hop.* ■ **The Gate (62)** 643 N. La Cienaga Blvd, West Hollywood, CA 90069 ☎ 310/289-8808 *Evening dress is important at this elegant first-rate nightclub.* ■ **Club Lingerie (63)** 6505 W. Sunset Blvd, Hollywood, CA 90038 ☎ 323/466-8557 *This comfortable disco-style establishment is split up into three zones, each devoted to a different type of music.*

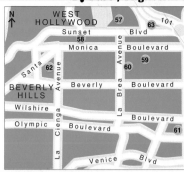

Television programs

To attend the recording of a broadcast, write to:
Audiences Unlimited *100 Universal City Plaza, Bldg 153, Universal City, CA 91608* ☎ *818/506-0067*

You can also make a reservation by calling the studios direct.
CBS-TV ☎ *323/852-2458*
NBC-TV ☎ *818/840-3537*
Paramount Pictures ☎ *323/956-5575*

 # What to see

Downtown L.A.

Discover the countless remarkable attractions of Downtown L.A. on foot. Choose from 11 guided themed tours. Reservation essential.
L.A. Conservancy Tours
☎ *213/621-2489*
◷ *Sat. 10am*
● *$8*

Festivals

Hundreds of cultural, ethnic and artistic events take place throughout the year. Consult the *L.A. Weekly* or the *Los Angeles Times* to find out details, or contact:
L.A. Convention & Visitors Bureau ☎ *213/689-8822*
Some dates:
January 1 Tournament of the Roses at Pasadena ☎ *818/419-7673*
Last weekend of July Malibu Art Festival, Malibu ☎ *310/456-9025*
October 31 Halloween Party, West Hollywood (on Santa Monica Blvd)

Movie Stars' Hor

A 2- to 4-hour bus tour in Beverly Hills and Bel-A to catch a glimpse of the movie stars' homes.
Trolleywood Tours
☎ *323/469-8184* ● *$31*
LA Tours
☎ *323/96-6793* ● *$42*

Los Angeles seen...

...from the sky Fly over Beverly Hills, Hollywood and Downtown in a helicopter, and finish off the evening with a candlelit dinner.
HeliUSA ☎ *310/641-9494 ● $99 for about 20 mins; including dinner $129*
...from a hearse Discover the hidden face of the City of Angels: tawdry tales, suspicious or unusual deaths. Over 80 locations.
Grave Line Tours ☎ *323/469-4149 ● $44 per 'body' (about two-and-a-half hours)*

74
Sights

For over 200 years, the towns of the Los Angeles district have been spreading out within a basin bounded by the Coastal Ranges to the east and, to the west, the Pacific Ocean. The City of Angels, world capital of movies and the home of everything outrageous, offers a rich cultural and architectural heritage that you should take the time to discover.

What to see

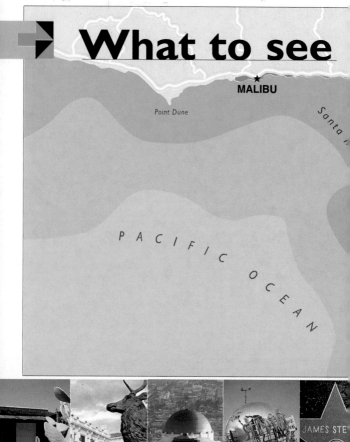

MALIBU

Point Dune

Santa

PACIFIC OCEAN

(6) ➡ 88   (17) ➡ 92   (24) ➡ 94   (27) ➡ 96   (37) ➡ 98

JAMES STE

El Pueblo de Los Angeles ➡ 88
Historic birthplace of Los Angeles, this Hispano-Mexican village boasts the oldest house in the town, on bustling Olvera Street.
Huntington Library ➡ 92
All the treasures

of the rail magnate formed into a collection in his luxurious home: rare books and manuscripts, English paintings and 15 gardens.
Griffith Observatory ➡ 94
Built on Mount Hollywood in the biggest urban park

in the United States, the observatory has dominated the city since 1935. An exceptional view over L.A. and the 'Hollywood' sign.
Universal Studios ➡ 96
A Technicolor voyage into the magic world of the seventh art.

Some 500 sets and disaster simulations guaranteed to send a shiver down your spine.
Walk of Fame ➡ 98
On Hollywood Boulevard, over 2,000 marble stars form a constellation to honor the

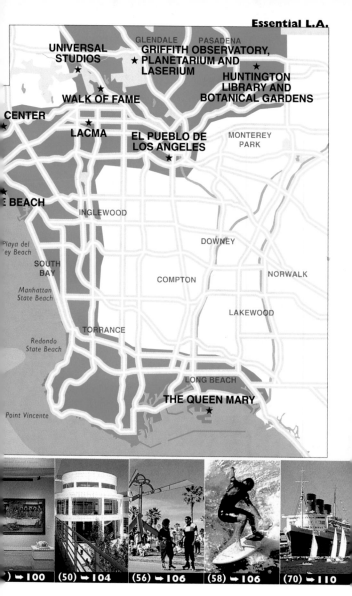

⇨ 100	(50) ⇨ 104	(56) ⇨ 106	(58) ⇨ 106	(70) ⇨ 110

celebrities of the entertainment world.

L.A. County Museum of Art ⇨ 100
One of the most important art museums in the United States. Renowned for its collections of European paintings, Islamic art, sculptures and decorative arts.

Getty Center ⇨ 104
The 'American Acropolis' houses the art collection of the oil magnate J. Paul Getty.

Venice Beach ⇨ 106
Frequented from the very start by representatives of the American counter-culture, this seaside town continues to promote the cliche of L.A. as laid back, creative and out of time.

Malibu ⇨ 106
Famous for its surf and its concentration of movie stars' homes, earning it the nickname *The Malibu Motion Picture Colony*.

The Queen Mary ⇨ 110
The largest luxury liner ever built (1934) moored for the last time at Long Beach in 1967. It now serves as a hotel ⇨ 34.

In the area
➥ **Where to stay:** ➥ 16
➥ **Where to eat:** ➥ 38 ➥ 40
➥ **After dark:** ➥ 74
➥ **Where to shop:** ➥ 128

What to see

Union Station (1)
100 N. Alameda Street, Los Angeles, CA 90012 ☎ 213/683-6875

One of the country's great train depots built by the Southern Pacific,
Union Pacific and Santa Fe Railroads in 1939, the massive cream-colored
structure is a mix of Spanish Colonial Revival, Mexican, Art Deco and
Moorish-style architecture.

Wells Fargo History Museum (2)
333 S. Grand Avenue, Los Angeles, CA 90071 ☎ 213/253-7166

(3rd St.) 🕐 *Mon.–Fri. 9am–5pm; closed public holidays* ● *free*

Return to the exciting days of the California Gold Rush. See an original
Concord Stagecoach built in 1897, an early Wells Fargo office, an
impressive display of gold samples and early photos tracing the history
of Wells Fargo Bank from its founding in 1852 up through today.

Museum of Contemporary Art (MoCA) (3)
250 S. Grand Avenue, Los Angeles, CA 90012 ☎ 213/626-6222

(2nd St.) 🅿 ▬ 🕐 *Tue.,Wed., Fri.–Sun. 11am–5pm; Thu. 11am–8pm; closed
Thanksgiving, Christmas, New Year* ● *$6; under-12s free; over-65s $4* ▦

East meets west in this stunning seven-level edifice of red sandstone and
grand pyramidal skylights designed by Irata Isozaki. The galleries are
devoted mostly to western art from the 1940s to the present and
exhibitions of art, photographs, sculpture and architecture. In the
permanent collection are the works of Jackson Pollock, Robert
Rauschenberg, Andy Warhol and Diane Arbus among many others.

Japanese American National Museum (4)
369 E. 1st Street, Los Angeles, CA 90012 ☎ 213/625-0414

(N. Central Ave) 🅿 ▬ 🕐 *Sun.,Tue.,Wed., Fri., Sat. 10am–5pm; Thu. 10am–8pm*
● *$6; under 17s $3; over-60s $5* ▦

The first U.S. museum dedicated to preserving the cultural identity of
Americans of Japanese ancestry. Through a collection of more than
30,000 objects from artifacts, paintings, works on paper, photography to
film, textiles and recorded oral histories.

Not forgetting

■ **Museum of Neon Art (5)** 501 W. Olympic Blvd, Los Angeles, CA
90015 ☎ 213/489-9918 *This unique museum traces the history of neon, electric
and kinetic in all its forms.* ■ **Avila Adobe House (6)** El Pueblo de Los
Angeles, 10 Olvera St., Los Angeles, CA 90012 ☎ 213/628-1274 *This
dilapidated house, built in 1818, is located in the earliest Los Angeles colony,
founded in 1781.* ■ **L.A. Children Museum (7)** 310 N. Main St., Los
Angeles, CA 90012 ☎ 213/687-8801 *An interactive universe where children are
introduced to the arts and sciences through play.* ■ **Bradbury Building
(8)** 304 S. Broadway, Los Angeles, CA 90012 ☎ 213/626-1893 *The magnificent
courtyard, skylights and open cage elevator of the 1893 office building were in
such films as Bladerunner and Lethal Weapon.* ■ **Angel Flight (9)** 351 S.
Hill St., Los Angeles, CA 90012 *This very short rack railway enables you to reach
the top of Bunker Hill for 25¢.*

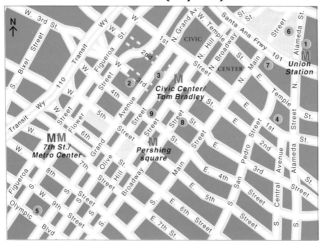

The City of Angels was founded in what is now the El Pueblo de Los Angeles Historical Monument in Downtown L.A. Today, its commercial hub is sprinkled with fine cultural attractions and diverse architecture. The cityscape's soaring mirrored glass and polished steel buildings are interspersed with historical Beaux Arts and Spanish-style landmarks.

In the area
- ➡ Where to stay: ➡ 16
- ➡ Where to eat: ➡ 38 ➡ 40
- ➡ After dark: ➡ 74
- ➡ Where to shop: ➡ 128

What to see

The Natural History Museum of L.A. County (10)
900 Exposition Boulevard, Los Angeles, CA 90007 ☎ 213/763-3466

(Vermont Ave) ▣ ◷ *Mon.–Fri. 9.30am–5pm; Sat., Sun. 10am–5pm; closed public holidays* ● *$8; under-5s free; under-12s $2; students, over-60s $5.50* ▣ ▦

Shades of *Jurassic Park*... View the gigantic skeletons of Tyrannosaurus Rex and Triceratops housed in a 1913 Spanish Renaissance building. More than 33 million diverse specimens and artifacts make up exhibits on science, history and culture, mammals, dinosaurs and insects. Also more than 2,000 gem and mineral specimens can be seen at the largest natural and historical museum in the Western United States. The hands on Discovery Center offers interactive education where children may dig for fossils and examine animal skins and skulls.

California African American Museum (11)
Exposition Park, 600 State Drive, Los Angeles, CA 90037 ☎ 213/744-7432

(S. Figueroa St.) ▣ *$3* ▣ ◷ *Tue.–Sun. 10am–5pm* ● *free* ▦

Finished just in time for the Los Angeles Summer Olympics of 1984, this museum of African-American Art focuses on art after 1930 (Harlem Renaissance), on the landscape painters of the 19th century, and on sculpture and photography, as well as multimedia subjects. Apart from the numerous temporary exhibitions, in the permanent collection you can find fertility figurines, funerary statues and ceremonial robes and masks.

California Science Center (12)
Exposition Park, 700 State Drive, Los Angeles, CA 90037 ☎ 213/744-7400

(S. Figueroa St.) ▣ *$5* ▣ ◷ *museum daily 10am–5pm; closed Thanksgiving, Christmas, New Year* ● *free* ◷ *IMAX variable* ● *$6.50; under-12s $3.75; students, over-60s $5 (+$1 for 3D movies)* ▣ ▦

Meet Tess, the 50-foot animatronic star of BodyWorks, demonstrating how body organs work together. Ride a high-wire bicycle to learn about gravity or build a structure to see how an earthquake would affect it. A tribute to flight, the Aerospace Hall features fighter planes, spacecraft and a 1920s glider. These, and other fascinating state-of-the-art interactive educational exhibits relating to science in everyday life, are presented in this hi-tech museum. The adjoining IMAX theater features spectacular larger-than-life entertaining educational movies making viewers feel like part of the action.

Not forgetting
■ **Fisher's Gallery (13)** University of South California, 823 Exposition Blvd, Los Angeles, CA 90089 ☎ 213/740-4561 *This gem of a gallery presents exhibitions ranging from antiquities and old masters through contemporary works by local, national and international artists.*

Downtown (Exposition Park) C D3

Exposition Park's famous seven-acre Rose Gardens separates the University of Southern California's campus from one of the city's most varied museum complexes featuring the sciences, the art of African Americans and natural history. Nearby, the Los Angeles Memorial Coliseum, built in 1923, hosted two Olympic Games in 1932 and 1984 and currently is home to the University of Southern California Trojan football team.

91

In the area
- **Where to stay:** ➡ 18
- **Where to eat:** ➡ 42 ➡ 56
- **After dark:** ➡ 78
- **Where to shop:** ➡ 130

What to see

Gamble House (14)
4 Westmoreland Place, Pasadena, CA 91103 ☎ 626/793-3334

(N. Orange Grove) 🅿 🕐 *Thu.–Sun. 12am–3pm* 🚌 *every 20 mins* ● *$5; under-12s free; students $3; over-60s $4* 🏛 *Tue.–Sat. 10am–5pm; Sun. 11.30am–5pm*

Pasadena's most famous architectural team, Greene & Greene, designed this for David and Mary Gamble, heirs to the Proctor & Gamble fortune, in 1908. Its original furniture, exotic hand-rubbed woods and inlays, leaded glass windows and Tiffany stained-glass door are well worth a visit.

Pasadena Historical Museum (15)
470 W. Walnut Street, Pasadena, CA 91103 ☎ 626/577-1660

(3rd St.) 🕐 *Thu.–Sun. 1pm–4pm; closed on public holidays* ● *$4; under-12s free; students, over-60s $3* 🚌 *1pm, 2pm, 3pm* 🏛

What was once the Feynes family estate now includes the History Center building, the 1905 beaux arts-style Feynes Mansion and the Finnish Folk Art Museum. The Center houses archival collections of more than one million historic photographs, rare books, manuscripts, maps, architectural records, and collections relating to the history of Pasadena.

Norton Simon Museum (16)
411 W. Colorado Boulevard, Pasadena, CA 91105 ☎ 626/449-6840

(Orange Grove) 🕐 *Wed., Thu., Sat., Sun. noon–6pm; Fri. noon–9pm; closed Thanksgiving, Dec. 25, Jan. 1* ● *$6; students, under-18s free; over-60s $3*

Seven centuries of extraordinary European art by world-famous artists including several Rodin sculptures and a vast collection of paintings, sculptures and pastels by Degas. The museum also boasts a celebrated Impressionist and Post-Impressionist collection and the works of Rembrandt, Goya and Picasso in addition to those of Kandinsky, Klee, Feininger and Jawlensky.

Huntington Library & Botanical Gardens (17)
1151 Oxford Road, San Marino, CA 91108 ☎ 626/405-2100

(Orlando Rd) 🕐 *Tue.–Fri. noon–4.30pm; Sat., Sun. 10.30am–4.30pm; closed on public holidays* ● *$8.50; under-12s free; students $6; over-60s $8* 🍴 🏛

Originally built as a home by railroad tycoon Henry E. Huntington in the early 1900s. The Library houses more than 600,000 books and 300 manuscripts including a Gutenberg bible, John Audubon's *The Birds of America* and a collection of early Shakespeare editions. The Gallery includes paintings of Reynolds, Mary Cassatt and Remington, Gainsborough's original *Blue Boy* and *Pinkie* by Lawrence.

Not forgetting

■ **Pacific Asian Museum (18)** 46 N. Los Robles Avenue, Pasadena, CA 91103 ☎ 626/449-2742 *Grace Nicholson's collection of Chinese art is kept in this pagoda-style museum.* ■ **City Hall (19)** 100 N. Garfield Ave, Pasadena, CA 91103 *This Italian Renaissance Revival building from 1927 has a crown-like dome rising 206 feet above the ground.* ■ **Wrigley Mansion (20)** 391 Orange Grove Blvd, Pasadena, CA 91184 ☎ 626/449-4100 *This 1906 Italianate mansion built by chewing gum magnate, William Wrigley Jr., is headquarters for the Rose Parade.*

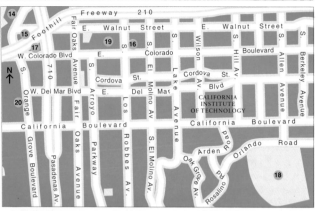

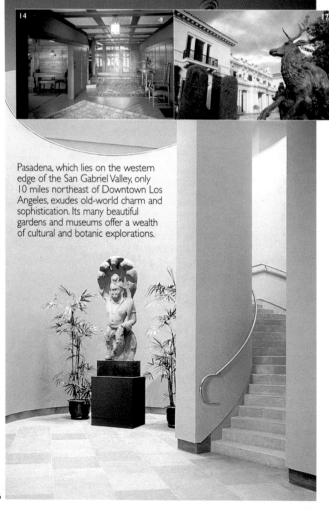

Pasadena, which lies on the western edge of the San Gabriel Valley, only 10 miles northeast of Downtown Los Angeles, exudes old-world charm and sophistication. Its many beautiful gardens and museums offer a wealth of cultural and botanic explorations.

The 4,107 acre park was named after its donor, Col. Griffith J. Griffith, a Welsh emigrant who struck gold in California. One of the largest parks in the country, it includes recreational facilities, educational and cultural complexes, attractions and wilderness. To find out what to do in the park, contact the **Griffith Park Ranger Station** ☎ *323/665-5188*.

 # What to see

Travel Town (21)
5200 W. Zoo Drive, Los Angeles, CA 90027 ☎ 323/662-5874

(Frwy 134) **P** 🌙 *Mon.–Fri. 10am–4pm; Sat., Sun. 10am–5pm; closed Dec. 25* ● *free* 🗂 🍴 *on reservation* ☎ *323/662-5874* 🎫

An open-air facility where children may climb on and 'drive' antique trains. Old cars and fire trucks displayed.

Los Angeles Zoo (22)
5333 Zoo Drive, Los Angeles, CA 90027 ☎ 323/644-6400

(Crystal Springs Dr.) 🚌 MTA 96 **P** ▤ 🌙 *daily 10am–5pm; closed Dec. 25* ● *$8.25; under-12s $3.25; over-60s $5.25* 🗂 🎫

The 113-acre home to more than 1,200 animals, in simulated habitats, is divided by geographical regions. Highlights include the Koala House, Great Ape Forest, Walk Through Aviary and the Reptile House featuring some of the world's most exotic creatures.

Autry Museum of Western Heritage (23)
4700 Western Heritage Dr., Los Angeles, CA 90027 ☎ 323/667-2000

(Zoo Dr.) 🚌 MTA 96 **P** ▤ 🌙 *Tue.–Sun. 10am–5pm; closed Thanksgiving, Dec. 25* ● *$7.50; under-12s $3; students, over-60s $5* 🍴 *on reservation* 🗂 🎫

One of the most comprehensive repositories of Western history in the world, the colorful Autry Museum pays homage to the American West – from its Native American roots to its pioneering past and the romance created by Hollywood. The collection includes more than 50,000 objects featuring fine art, folk art, artifacts and archival materials.

Griffith Observatory, Planetarium & Laserium (24)
2800 E. Observatory Road, Los Angeles, CA 90027 ☎ 323/664-1191

🚌 LC203 **P** ▤ 🌙 *Observatory and Science Center Sep.–May: Tue.–Fri. 2–10pm; Sat., Sun. 12.30–10pm/June–Aug.: daily 12.30–10pm; closed Columbus Day, Thanksgiving, Dec. 25* ● *free* 🌙 *Planetarium Sep.–May: Tue.–Fri. 3–7.30pm; Sat., Sun. 1.30pm, 3pm, 4.30pm, 7.30pm/June–Aug.: Mon.–Fri. 1.30pm, 3pm, 7.30pm; Sat., Sun. 1.30pm, 3pm, 4.40pm, 7.30pm* ● *$4; under-12s $2; over-65s $3* 🌙 *Laserium variable* ● *$8; under-12s, over-65s $7* 🎫 ⛷

Visitors get a lesson in astronomy and see a telescope for stargazing, globes, meteorite collection, spacecraft and telescope models, live images of the sun, a working seismograph measuring the area's constant movement and astronomy computer games. The Planetarium theater has live multimedia presentations using over 100 special-effect projectors and the Laserium offers symphonies and ballets of light and sound.

Not forgetting

■ **Forest Lawn Hollywood Hills (25)** 6300 Forest Lawn Dr., Los Angeles, CA 90068 *Jean Harlow, Errol Flynn, Nat King Cole, Clark Gable and Carole Lombard are among the many stars buried in this cemetery, satirized by Evelyn Waugh in The Loved One.* ■ **Hollywood Sign (26)** *Erected on Mount Lee in 1923, these nine magical letters were originally thirteen, advertising Hollywoodland, a real estate development. Approach it from Mount Lee Drive, but you'll see it best from the observatory.*

Paramount is the only studio left in Hollywood but a quick drive to Burbank or Culver City lets you in on some moviemaking secrets in behind-the-scene studio tours at Warner Brothers or Sony Studios or even a theme park experience at Universal.

➔ What to see

Universal Studios Tour (27)
100 Universal City Plaza, Universal City, CA 91608 ☎ 818/508-9600

(Fwy 101) 🅿 🕐 *daily: summer 10am–10pm; winter 10am–7pm; closed Thanksgiving, Dec. 25* ● *$39; under-12s $29; over-60s $34* 🆔 🏢 *Universal City Walk* ➥ *126*

Join the spectacle and atmosphere of some of the screen's most acclaimed motion picture and TV productions. This is, in fact, a perfect small amusement park. The Backlot Tour tram takes you by current directors' bungalows, to an exterior set for *Jaws*, past the Bates motel in *Psycho* into dark sound stages to experience thrilling moments with *King Kong* and *Earthquake*. Hundreds of exterior sets transport the visitor into the legendary Old West, New York and Europe. There are six shows and five rides celebrating such films as *E.T.* for a bike trip into the night skies or *Jurassic Park* with a boat trip into the prehistoric past.

Warner Bros VIP Tour (28)
4000 Warner Boulevard, Burbank, CA 91522 ☎ 818/954-1744

(W. Olive Ave) 🅿 🕐 *Mon.–Fri. 9am–3pm* 🎫 *Summer: Sat. 10am, 2pm* ● *$30*

An enlightening look at the moviemaking process, the personal two-hour golf-cart and walking tour includes a visit to one of the largest costume departments in the world, exterior sets and recording stages, sound stages and prop rooms. The studio museum houses 75 years of studio artifacts from classic films. Children under 8 are not admitted.

Sony Pictures Studio Tour (29)
10202 W. Washington Blvd, Culver City, CA 90232 ☎ 323/520-8687

(Overland Ave) 🅿 🕐 *Mon.–Fri. 9am–5pm; closed on public holidays* ● *$20*

A tour of this working studio offers a rare glimpse of Old Hollywood's glory days, a peek at current movie and TV-making and a preview of hi-tech movie innovations on the horizon. See where *Men in Black* battled outlaw aliens and take a walk on the Yellow Brick Road.

Paramount Pictures Studios (30)
5555 Melrose Avenue, Hollywood, CA 90046 ☎ 323/956-1777

(N. Van Ness Ave) 🅿 🕐 *Mon.–Fri. 9am–2pm; closed on public holidays ● $20*

Strictly speaking, the only studio in Hollywood proper. The majestic gate on the corner of Bronson Avenue took its place in the history of the movies when Gloria Swanson passed through it in the film *Sunset Boulevard* (1950). There are two-hour guided tours round the sets of this historic studio (small groups of over-10s only).

Not forgetting
■ **NBC Studio Tour** (31) 3000 W. Alameda Ave, Burbank, CA 91523 ☎ 818/840-3537 *A 70-minute tour which gives you an insight into the world of television. Admission to live recordings is free, but tickets should be reserved in advance. Gift shop.*

In the area

- **Where to stay:** ➡ 20
- **Where to eat:** ➡ 44
- **After dark:** ➡ 68 ➡ 70 ➡ 74 ➡ 76 ➡ 78 ➡ 80
- **Where to shop:** ➡ 132 ➡ 134

What to see

Edmund D. Edelman Hollywood Bowl Museum (32)
2301 N. Highland Avenue, Los Angeles, CA 90068 ☎ 323/850-2058

(Cahuenga Blvd) 🅿 *free before 4.30pm* 🕐 *Tue.–Sat. 10am–4pm (8.30pm on concert evenings)* ● *free* 📷 📹 *on reservation ☎ 323/662-5874* ♿

A fascinating archive of photographs, videos, architectural renderings, memorabilia from every concert that has taken place in the stunning concert shell whose balloon-shaped seating was designed by Myron Hunt in 1926; Elliott, Bowen and Walz built the shell completed in 1929.

Hollywood Entertainment Museum (33)
7021 Hollywood Boulevard, Hollywood, CA 90028 ☎ 323/465-7900

(Sycamore St.) 🅿 🕐 *Sep. 15–June 15: Mon., Tue., Thu.–Sun. 11am–4pm; June 16–Sep. 14: daily 10am–4pm* ● *$7.50; under-12s $4; students, over-65s $4.50* ♿

The museum pays homage to both the old and new Hollywood, beginning with silent films. You can go on the set of *Cheers* or *Star Trek* and test your voice in a recording studio. There is plenty of memorabilia, a gift shop and a restaurant.

Mann's Chinese Theater (34)
6925 Hollywood Boulevard, Hollywood, CA 90028 ☎ 323/461-3331

(N. Orchid Dr.) 🅿 🕐 *movie theater* ➡ 74

This Hollywood landmark is famous for its wildly ornate Chinese-inspired façade and its courtyard's 205 large cement squares are inscribed with the signatures and the hand and footprints of major Hollywood stars dating from 1927, when movie star Norma Talmadge accidentally stepped onto a sidewalk of wet cement, to the present.

Hollywood Wax Museum (35)
6767 Hollywood Boulevard, Hollywood, CA 90028 ☎ 323/462-5991

(Highland Blvd) 🕐 *Mon.–Fri. 10am–midnight; Sat., Sun. 10am–1am* ● *$9.95; under-12s $5.95; over-65s $7.95* ♿

Scenes from great classics such as *The Wizard of Oz* and *Austin Powers*, life-like figurines of stars from the world of cinema, sport and politics, as well as a Chamber of Horrors and a reconstruction of the Last Supper.

Not forgetting

■ **Ripley's Believe It or Not (36)** 6780 Hollywood Blvd, Hollywood, CA 90028 ☎ 323/466-6335 *An astonishing collection of curios from all over the world.* ■ **Walk of Fame (37)** Hollywood Blvd, Hollywood, CA 90028 *Since 1958, more than 2,000 celebrities have been immortalized on the sidewalks with terrazzo and brass embedded stars sporting their name; most visited are those of Marilyn Monroe (1644 Hollywood Blvd), John Lennon (1750 Vine St.) and Elvis Presley (6777 Hollywood Blvd).* ■ **Hollywood History Museum (38)** 1660 N. Highland, Hollywood, CA 90028 ☎ 323/464-7776 *This Art-Deco gem used to house Max Factor cosmetics. It now tells the story of the movie and television industries and, of course, that of Max Factor.* ■ **Capitol Records Building (39)** 1750 Vine St., Hollywood, CA 90028 ☎ 323/462-6252 *This landmark tower that looks like a stack of records designed by Welton Becket & Associates in 1954 has a rooftop beacon that flashes the word Hollywood in Morse code at night.*

The old queen of glamor has severely declined over the last two decades, but a facelift to the tune of several million dollars should return her to her former glory and give her back the Oscars ceremony. In the meantime, her kitsch attractions and her movie museums continue to fascinate the public. Giving a taste of her glorious past: the Hollywood Heritage Museum (*2100 N. Highland Ave*) has been set up in the first-ever studio.

36

What to see

George C. Page Museum / La Brea Tar Pits (40)
5801 Wilshire Boulevard, Los Angeles, CA 90036 ☎ 323/857-6311

(S. Curson Ave) 🕐 *Mon.–Fri. 6.30am–5pm; Sat., Sun. 10am–5pm; closed on public holidays, Mon. in summer* ● *$6; under-10s $2; students, over-60s $3.50* 🎟 *museum Wed.–Sun. 2pm / tar pits Wed.–Sun. 1pm* ♿

Fossils are still being found in the bubbly goo of the La Brea Tar Pits, the largest concentration of ice-age remains currently known. Bones of sloths, saber-tooth tigers, wolves and mammoths are displayed at the Page Museum. Visitors may view the glass-enclosed paleontology laboratory and also see Pepper's Ghosts, where through lighting and hologram-type techniques the bones of the La Brea Woman and a saber-tooth tiger appear to become covered with flesh; and in the summer, see paleontologists working in Pit 91.

Los Angeles County Museum of Art LACMA (41)
5905 Wilshire Boulevard, Los Angeles, CA 90036 ☎ 323/857-6000

(Ogden Dr.) 🅿 🕐 *Mon., Tue., Thu. noon–8pm; Fri. noon–9pm; Sat., Sun. 11am–8pm* ● *$7; under-17s $1; students, over-60s $5* 🎟 🎟 ♿

Los Angeles's largest county museum complex is six buildings containing a vast collection of paintings, sculptures, costumes, textiles and decorative arts; the world's largest collection of Indian, Nepalese and Tibetan art is housed in the Ahmanson Building; the Pavilion for Japanese Art highlights the famed Shin'enkan painting collection and the Southwestern museum annex features Native American and Southwestern art and artifacts.

Petersen Automotive Museum (42)
6060 Wilshire Boulevard, Los Angeles, CA 90036 ☎ 323/930-2277

(Fairfax Ave) 🅿 🕐 *Tue.–Sun. 10am–6pm; closed Thanksgiving, Dec. 25, Jan. 1* ● *$7; under-12s $3; students, over-60s $5*

The museum of automotive history shows the importance of the car in America but particularly in the culture and life of the Angelinos: the whole city bears their mark, as can be seen from the drive-ins, the malls and the billboards. Displayed on the second floor are racing and classic cars belonging to, or having belonged to, stars or movie studios.

Carole & Barry Kaye Museum of Miniatures (43)
5900 Wilshire Boulevard, Los Angeles, CA 90036 ☎ 323/937-6464

(Spaulding Ave) 🅿 *$4* 🕐 *Tue.–Sat. 10am–5pm; Sun. 11am–5pm; closed Dec. 25, Jan. 1* ● *$7.50; under-11s $3; under-21s $5; over-60s $6.50* ♿

The largest collection of miniatures in the world in this 14,000 square foot museum with vaulted ceilings will fascinate young and old alike. It includes the figures of the First Ladies in inaugural gowns, models of the Vatican, the *Titanic* and even the O. J. Simpson Trial.

Not forgetting
■ **Craft & Folk Art Museum (44)** 5800 Wilshire Boulevard, Los Angeles, CA 90036 ☎ 323/937-4230 *Occasional and traveling exhibitions of contemporary creations – handicrafts, design, popular and traditional art – from around the world.*

This part of the interminably long Wilshire Boulevard, the true center of commercial activity, was dubbed 'Miracle Mile' in the 1930s. The large number of museums of all sorts (art, natural history, automotive, miniatures) which are located there nowadays has earned it the new name of 'Museum Row'.

41

42

43

40

43

➡ What to see

Greystone Mansion (45)
905 Loma Vista Drive, Beverly Hills, CA 90210 ☎ 310/550-4796

(Doheny Rd) 🅿 🕒 *daily: Oct.–Mar. 10am–5pm; Apr.–Sep. 10am-6pm* ● *free*

The 46,000 square foot, 55-room Tudor manor, built by oil magnate Edward L. Doheny, is surrounded by 16 acres of lush landscaped balustraded terraces complete with pools and fountains. Gardens are open for strolling and picnicking but the mansion is closed to the public. It has been used as a location for such films as *The Witches of Eastwick* and *Ghostbusters II*.

Virginia Robinson Gardens (46)
1008 Elden Way, Beverly Hills, CA 90210 ☎ 310/276-5367

(N. Crescent Dr.) 🅿 ⬛ 🕒 *Tue., Wed., Fri.–Sun. 11am–5pm; Thu. 11am–8pm; closed Thanksgiving, Dec. 25, Jan. 1* ● *$8; students, over-60s $4*

The estate, built in 1911 as the home of the heirs to the J.W. Robinson Department Store chain, has a guided 1 hour 45 minute tour of the main residence, pool pavilion and more than six acres of landscaped grounds featuring five distinctive gardens: The Italian Terrace Garden, the Tropical Palm Garden, the Rose Garden, Kitchen Garden and Formal Mall Garden.

Museum of Television & Radio (47)
465 Beverly Drive, Beverly Hills, CA 90210 ☎ 310/786-1000

(S. Santa Monica Blvd) ⬛ 🕒 *Wed., Fri.–Sun. 10am–5pm; Thu. 11am–9pm; closed July 4, Thanksgiving, Dec. 25* ● *$6; under-12s $3; students, over-60s $4* 🈁

Designed by Getty Center architect, Richard Meier, the museum houses more than 100,000 television and radio programs which visitors may access. Covering over 70 years of broadcasting history, programs include news, public affairs, documentaries, drama, advertising, sports and comedy. Individual consoles enable you to listen to or view footage such as the Nixon–Kennedy debate of 1960, the legendary Ali versus Frazier boxing match (1974) or an interview with Marilyn Monroe from 1955. Private showings are organized in two movie theaters.

Museum of Tolerance (48)
9786 W. Pico Blvd, West Los Angeles, CA 90035 ☎ 310/553-9036

(Roxbury Dr.) 🅿 ⬛ 🕒 *Mon.–Thu. 10am–4pm; Fri. 10am–1pm; Sun. 11am–5pm; closed on public and Jewish holidays* ● *$8.50; under-10s $3.50; students $5.50; over-60s $6.50* 🎧 *in other languages* 🈁

Visitors are challenged to confront bigotry and racism at this unique 165,000 square foot interactive museum focusing on personal prejudice, group intolerance, the struggle for civil rights in America, 20th-century genocides and culminating in a major exhibition of the Holocaust.

Not forgetting

■ **Museum of Jurassic Technology (49)** 9341 Venice Blvd, Los Angeles, CA 90232 ☎ 310/836-6131 *A fascinating, eclectic, poetic exhibition that presents astounding natural or purely imaginary curiosities with the aim of making you fall in love with the Lower Jurassic period.*

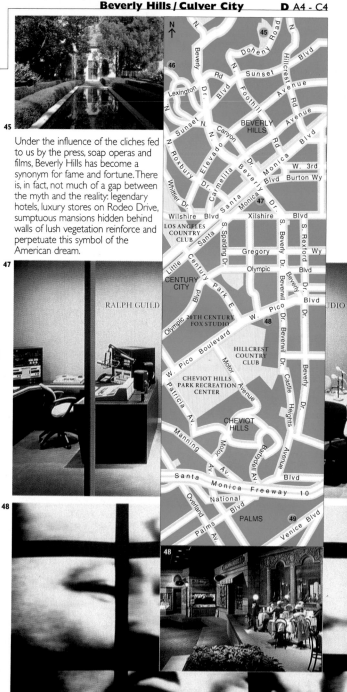

45

Under the influence of the cliches fed to us by the press, soap operas and films, Beverly Hills has become a synonym for fame and fortune. There is, in fact, not much of a gap between the myth and the reality: legendary hotels, luxury stores on Rodeo Drive, sumptuous mansions hidden behind walls of lush vegetation reinforce and perpetuate this symbol of the American dream.

47

48

What to see

The J. Paul Getty Museum at the Getty Center (50)
1200 Getty Center Drive, Los Angeles, CA 90049 ☎ 310/440-7360

(Getty Center Dr.) 🚍 561, SM 14 **P** $5 on reservation 🕐 Tue., Wed. 11am–7pm; Thu., Fri. 11am–9pm; Sat., Sun. 10am–6pm; closed on public holidays
● free ▢ ▦ ✦ ▨

This, the latest star in the galaxy of Los Angeles museums, and the work of architect Richard Meier, perches like a gleaming, white city on the heights of the Santa Monica Mountains. Four of the five one-story museum pavilions built around a paved courtyard are home to permanent collections, the fifth houses temporary exhibitions. These collections include Greek and Roman antiquities, illuminated manuscripts, sculptures, French furniture and decorative arts; European painting (14th-19th centuries) is seen to optimum effect as a result of a play of natural light, thanks to a judicious system of adjustable glass panels. In this way you can admire *Irises* by Van Gogh (1889), the *Young Italian Woman at a Table* by Cézanne and *Venus and Adonis* by Titian. You may stroll in the gardens, in particular the Central Garden, at the heart of which is a maze of azaleas that seems to float on a vast ornamental lake.

UCLA Fowler Museum of Cultural History (51)
405 Hilgard Avenue, Los Angeles, CA 90024 ☎ 310/825-4361

(Warner Ave) **P** $5 parking lots 4 and 5 on the campus 🕐 Wed., Fri.–Sun. noon–5pm; Thu. noon–8pm ● $5; students, over-60s $3 ▦

Considered to be one of the best university museums of anthropology in the country, it contains over 750,000 cultural, contemporary, historic and prehistoric objects. Items in the collection come from all five continents, with Africa particularly well represented, and they include weapons, jewelry, statuary and musical instruments.

Armand Hammer Museum of Art (53)
10899 Wilshire Boulevard, Westwood, CA 90024 ☎ 310/443-7000

(Westwood Blvd) **P** $2.75 ▭ 🕐 Tue., Wed., Fri., Sat. 11am–7pm; Thu. 11am–9pm; Sun. 11am–5pm; closed July 4, Thanksgiving, Dec. 25, Jan. 1 ● $4.50; under-17s free; students, over-60s $3 ▢ ▦

This big collection of Impressionist and Post-Impressionist paintings also includes works by Rembrandt, Raphael, and Sargent. Don't miss the 7,000 or so sculptures and lithographs by Honoré Daumier.

Not forgetting

■ **Westwood Village (52)** Wilshire & Westwood Blvds *Home to the largest concentration of first-run movie theaters in the world where blockbusters are often premiered, Westwood is excellent for strolling and people-watching; shops and restaurants abound. Developed in the 1920s, it boomed when UCLA opened in 1929.* ■ **Westwood Memorial Park (54)** 1218 Glendon Ave, Westwood, CA 90024 *This gem of funerary architecture, edged with majestic jacaranda trees, is the last resting-place of many celebrities including Marilyn Monroe, Natalie Wood, John Cassavetes and Frank Zappa.* ■ **UCLA (55)** 405 Hilgard Ave, Westwood, CA 90024 ☎ 213/825-4321 *The University of California at Los Angeles, founded in 1919, moved to its present quarters in 1929, and is a veritable city, with 36,500 students. It has produced four Nobel prize-winners and a filmmaker, Francis Ford Coppola.*

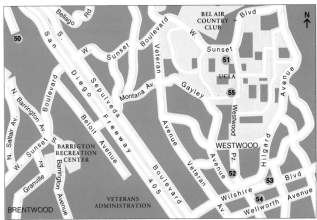

Marilyn Monroe, Joan Crawford, Shirley Temple, Raymond Chandler, Joan Didion and John Gregory Dunne have all lived in Brentwood, one of the most fashionable districts of L.A. Now the most famous local star is the Getty Center, opened in 1997. To the east you find Westwood Village, which has the greatest concentration of movie theaters in Los Angeles and is home to the prestigious UCLA.

Los Angeles County is edged by 75 miles of sea shore. A meeting place for Angelinos, a paradise for surfers and players of beach volleyball, the beaches are an integral part of the California lifestyle. And, for your safety, the lifeguards, made famous by the TV series *Baywatch*, keep an eye on your activities in the water from their watchtowers.

What to see

Malibu Lagoon & Surfrider Beach (56)
Pacific Coast Highway, Malibu, CA 90265 ☎ 310/456-9497

(Serra Rd) 🚏 434 🅿 *$6 Lifeguards* 🍴 🎦 🏢

Adjacent to the Malibu pier, Surfrider Beach, surfing capital in the 1950s and 1960s, still has the best waves in the area, especially at the end of summer after the storms in the southeast, when waves can reach 10 ft high. The Malibu Lagoon beach is quieter and has a bird sanctuary (guided tours at the weekend).

Will Rogers State Beach (57)
Pacific Coast Highway, Pacific Palisades, CA 90272 ☎ 310/394-3266

(Temescal Canyon Rd) 🚏 434 🅿 *Lifeguards*

This narrow stretch of sand is a favorite meeting place for families, drawn by the numerous activities such as beach volleyball. As the waves are less strong here, budding surfers can have a go in safety.

Santa Monica Beach (58)
Pacific Coast Highway, Santa Monica, CA 90401

(California Incline) 🚏 434 🅿 *$8 Lifeguards* 🍴 🎦 🏢

Along with Venice, Santa Monica remains synonymous with the 'surf and sun' culture of California, which explains its enormous popularity. This is also due to a wealth of sporting and leisure activities including volleyball, its games courts, and, not to be forgotten, the pier ➡ 108. There is an asphalt biking and skating strip along the beach, where you can rent skates, rollerblades and bicycles.

Venice City Beach (59)
Winward Avenue, Los Angeles, CA 90291

(Crystal Springs Dr.) 🚏 33, 436 🅿 *Lifeguards* 🍴 🎦 🏢

With its beach vendors, joggers, fire-eaters, Hare Krishnas, artists of every type and teeming crowds, the Venice Boardwalk looks at first glance like a very disreputable area. But this friendly beach is nonetheless a legend, in particular for Muscle Beach, an outdoor bodybuilding club. Indeed, it was here that the bodybuilding culture was born in the 1940s and 1950s. Take the time to stroll along the canals between Venice and Washington boulevards. These are the last remaining traces of a project begun in 1904 by Abbot Kinney, an attempt to recreate Venice in America, with gondolas and palaces included.

Not forgetting

■ **Manhattan Beach & Pier (60)** Manhattan Beach Blvd, Manhattan, CA 90266 *This beach and pier, running along the edge of a well-to-do seaside town, provides the setting for international surfing and volleyball competitions.*
■ **Abalone Cove (61)** Palos Verdes Dr. South, Rancho Palos Verdes, CA 90275 *The rocks here give you the chance to fish for sea urchins, scallops and abalone in the pools and forests of kelp. Make sure you also cross the road to visit the Wayfarer's Chapel by Frank Lloyd Wright.*
■ **Cabrillo Beach (62)** 6300 Forest Lawn Dr., Los Angeles, CA 90068 *Surfing, volleyball, boat and bicycle rental, and picnic areas with in-built barbecues.*

56

57

SANTA MONICA

58

59

INGLEWOOD

60 MANHATTAN BEACH

TORRANCE

61 LONG BEACH

62

Pacific

Santa Monica Bay

Ocean

N

59

56

59

BEACHWAY
FOR BICYCLISTS
AND OTHERS

USE WITH
COURTESY
AND
CAUTION

58

What to see

Santa Monica Museum of Art (63)
Bergamot Station, 2525 Michigan Avenue, Santa Monica, CA 90404 ☎ 310/586-6488

(Cloverfield Blvd) 🅿 ▬ 🕐 *Tue.–Sat. 11am–6pm; closed on public holidays ● $3; under-12s free; students, artists, over-60s $2* ⊞ @ *smmuseum@vip.com*

Known for exhibiting works by emerging and mid-career artists, particularly from Southern California, the museum has become a premier showcase for provocative visual arts programs and encouraging dialogue among people of diverse backgrounds and esthetic values.

Santa Monica Pier & Palisade Park (64)

(Colorado Blvd) 🅿 🕐 *Palisade Park Sun.–Thu. 10am–10pm; Fri., Sat. 10am–midnight ● free / UCLA Ocean Discovery Center summer: Tue.–Fri. 2pm–6pm; Sat. 11am–6pm; Sun. 11am–5pm / winter: Sat., Sun. 11am–5pm ● $3* 🍴 🖵 ⊞

The oldest pleasure pier on the west coast opened in 1909 and has an amusement ride center, UCLA Ocean Discovery Center and a handcrafted carousel circa 1922, as well as restaurants, arcades, shops. Adjacent is Palisade Park, a 26-acre cliff-top greenbelt that is a favorite place for strolling, sunning and picnicking. Just south of the Pier, the original, legendary Muscle Beach has reopened and a Chess Park serving 80 players has been installed.

Museum of Flying (65)
2772 Donald Douglas Loop North, Santa Monica, CA 90405 ☎ 213/626-6222

(28th St.) 🅿 ▬ 🕐 *Tue.–Sun. 10am–5pm ● $7 under-16s $3; over-60s $5* ⊞

Built on the site where Donald Douglas founded the Douglas Aircraft Company in 1922, this museum will introduce you to the history of aviation through its collection of legendary aircraft. Among them: the *New Orleans*, a Douglas World Cruiser from 1924, and one of the first planes to have flown around the world; a replica of the Fokker DR-1 triplane, made unforgettable by its pilot Manfred von Richthofen, the famous 'Red Baron'; or even the Bede BD-5J Micro (1973), the smallest jet in the world, used in the 1983 James Bond movie *Octopussy*.

Not forgetting
■ **Angel Attic Museum (66)** 516 Colorado Ave, Santa Monica, CA 90401 ☎ 310/394-8331 *Set in a Victorian house, this museum returns you to the wonderful world of childhood. Miniature colonial mansions and southern plantations, old dolls houses, dolls and toys of all sorts.* ■ **The Getty Villa (67)** 17985 Pacific Coast Highway, Malibu, CA 90265 *A replica of the Roman villa of Papiri, the home of the oil magnate J. Paul Getty has a collection of Roman, Greek and Egyptian art.* ■ **California Heritage Museum (68)** 2612 Main St., Santa Monica, CA 90405 ☎ 310/392-8537 *This residence was built in 1894 on Ocean Blvd for Roy Jones, son of the founder of the town, Senator John Percival Jones. Restored and moved to its current location, it houses temporary exhibitions devoted to the decorative arts, as well as to Californian architecture and history.*

67

66

65

64

Novelist Raymond Chandler immortalized Santa Monica as 'Bay City' in his brilliant Philip Marlowe stories. At the Pacific end of the original Route 66, this popular beachfront resort town lures sun lovers to the sand and surf during summer months. Many museums, art galleries, the high-energy Third Street Promenade and the colorful Santa Monica Pier provide a bustling scene.

In the area
 Where to stay: ➡ 34
 Where to eat: ➡ 56 ➡ 64
 After dark: ➡ 8
 Where to shop: ➡ 126

➤ What to see

Long Beach Aquarium of the Pacific (69)
100 Aquarium Way, Rainbow Harbor, Long Beach,
CA 90802 ☎ 562/590-3100

(W. Shoreline Dr.) Ⓜ *Transit Mall* 🅿 ▭ 🕐 *daily 9am–6pm; closed Dec. 25*
● *$14.95; under-12s $7.95; over-60s $11.95* 🔳 ▢ *Cafe Scuba* 🔲

This world-class aquarium allows visitors to walk through plexi-glass tunnels surrounded by sharks and tropical fish. More than 12,000 ocean animals representing over 500 species in 17 major living habitats and 30 focus exhibits are displayed. See giant octopuses, endangered sea turtles of Baja, sea lions of Santa Catalina and diving birds. Special hands-on areas allow guests to handle many of the sea creatures. Shows scheduled throughout the day.

The Queen Mary (70)
1126 Queens Highway, Long Beach, CA 90802 ☎ 562/435-3511

(Queens Way) 🅿 ▭ 🕐 *daily 10am–6pm* ● *$15; under-12s $9; over-60s $13*
🔳 🔲 ▢ 🔲

The *Queen Mary* was one of the world's most luxurious ocean liners. Visitors may take a self-guided or guided tour to explore the ship from the wheelhouse to the engine room, and view officer's quarters, WW II exhibits, original table settings and watch a film with the original footage of the launch of the ship and the time when she served as a troop ship. The liner shares its harbor home with another maritime phenomenon, the Soviet-built Foxtrot-class submarine Povodnaya Lodka B-427, also known as Scorpion, commissioned during the height of the cold war.

Long Beach Museum of Art (71)
2300 E. Ocean Boulevard, Long Beach, CA 90803 ☎ 562/439-2119

(Kennebec Ave) 🅿 ▭ 🕐 *Museum Tue.–Sun. 11am–7pm / Gardens Tue.–Sun. 7.30am–7pm* ● *$5; under-12s free; students, over-62s $4* 🔲 ▢

Overlooking the beach, this 1912 Craftsman-style carriage house has housed a permanent collection of paintings and sculptures by contemporary Southern Californian artists since 1950. The museum organizes exhibitions featuring the experimental projects of people working in multimedia.

Not forgetting

■ **Museum of Latin American Art (MoLAA) (72)** 628 Alamitos Avenue, Long Beach, CA 90814 ☎ 562/437-1689 *This shows Latin American art since WW II and has a Latin American restaurant.*
■ **Naples (73)** E. 2nd St., Long Beach, CA 90803 *This mainly residential island is the work of A. M. Parsons who, just like Abbot Kinney and his Venice* ➡ *106, invested in marshy ground to recreate a city on a lagoon.*
■ **Getaway Gondola (74)** 5437 E. Ocean Blvd, Long Beach, CA 90803 ☎ 562/437-1689 *It's not only in Venice that you find gondolas: a one-hour trip on the canals is a romantic way to visit the island. Closed on Mondays.*

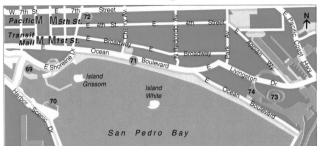

W 7th St. E 7th Street
Pacific M M 5th St. E 4th St E 4th Street E Pacific Coast Hwy
Transit M M 1st St. E Broadway E Broadway Appian Hwy
Mall E Ocean E 71 Boulevard E Livingston Dr. 74 73
69 E Shoreline Dr. Island Island Ocean Boulevard
70 Grissom White
Harbor Scenic Dr.

San Pedro Bay

N

Cherry Av. Redondo Av. Park Av.

70

73

The second-largest city in Los Angeles County, Long Beach has, in the last few years, become a popular destination showcasing a grand old ship and a state-of-the-art aquarium. It is home to several popular annual events including the Toyota Grand Prix auto races which take place each spring and the Blues Festival held over the Labor Day weekend in September.

70

69

Further afield

The wine trail

About 20,000 acres of vineyards grow in the Santa Ynez range to the north of Santa Barbara. Follow the Foxen Canyon Wine Trail and taste the Viogniers, Chardonnays and Cabernets. To receive the full list of wines, call: *Santa Barbara Vintners' Association* ☎ *805/688-0881 or 800/218-0881*

Death Valley

Deserts of salt (Devil's Golf Course), canyons (Golden Canyon), palm groves (Furnace Creek) are examples of the splendid scenery offered by a trip across Death Valley (especially at dawn or dusk when the rocks become tinged with color). Some 200 miles north of L.A., this national park, 282 ft below sea level, is best visited in April (in summer the temperature reaches well over 100°F).
Furnace Creek Visitor Center ☎ *619/786-2331* 🕐 *daily 8am-5pm*

Golf at Palm Springs

With over 90 greens, the Palm Springs hot spa has become the world's golfing capital (two hours' drive from Los Angeles). This is a retreat that proves very popular with Angelinos during the wintertime. You can also ski on Mount Jacinto by taking the Aerial Tramway, a cable car that enables you to pass from the desert to the cool of snow-covered peaks in 20 minutes.

23
Days out

Skiing at Big Bear Lake

The resort at Big Bear Lake (84 miles from L.A.), in the heart of the mountains which close off the Los Angeles basin, offers a host of physical activities throughout the year: sailing, fishing, mountain biking, hiking, jet-skiing, snowboarding, cross-country or downhill skiing…

Big Bear Lake Visitors Center
630 Bartlet Road, Village ☎ *800/424-4232* ➠ *909/866-5671*
🕒 *Mon.–Fri. 8am–5pm; Sat., Sun. 9am–5pm*

Gambling in Las Vegas

Five hours' drive to the northeast of Los Angeles, Las Vegas is the realm of show- biz and casinos. Consult the *L.A. Times* for unbeatable weekly special offers (inclusive of hotel and flight).
Las Vegas Visitor Center
Convention Center, 3150 Paradise Rd, Nevada
☎ *702/892-7575*

INDEX BY TYPE

Architecture
Crystal Cathedral
➠ 120
El Presidio ➠ 118
Mission Santa
Barbara ➠ 118
Santa Barbara
County Court-
house ➠ 118

Beaches
Balboa Island &
Peninsula ➠ 120
Laguna Beach
➠ 120

Museums
Bowers Museum
➠ 120
Irvine Museum
➠ 120
Mission Santa
Barbara ➠ 118
Movieland Wax
Museum ➠ 120
Orange County
Museum of Art
➠ 120
Santa Barbara
Historical
Museum ➠ 118
Santa Barbara
Maritime
Museum ➠ 118
Santa Barbara
Museum of Art
➠ 118

Theme parks, attractions
Disneyland ➠ 116
Hobby & Adven-
ture City ➠ 116
Hurricane Harbor
➠ 116
Knott's Berry
Farm ➠ 116
Movieland Wax
Museum ➠ 120
Santa Barbara
Winery ➠ 118
Six Flags Magic
Mountain ➠ 116
Wild Rivers
➠ 116

Places of interest, nature reserves
Balboa Island &
Peninsula ➠ 120
Catalina Island
➠ 122
Channel Islands
➠ 122
Crystal Cathedral
➠ 120
El Presidio ➠ 118
Laguna Beach
➠ 120
Mission Santa
Barbara ➠ 118
Santa Barbara
Botanic Garden
➠ 118

Viewpoint
County
Courthouse
➠ 118

The directions given indicate the highway to take on leaving Downtown Los Angeles. If you have no car, you can choose whether to use MTA buses ➡ 10, *Metrolink* commuter trains ➡ from Union Station ➡ 8 or, for the theme parks, the shuttle services provided by numerous hotels.

Further afield

San Francisco

101

SANTA BARBARA COUNTY

Pt. Conception

Isla Vista

7 14

Santa Barbara

Santa Barbara Channel

101

Ventura

Oxnar

San Miguel Island

22

CHANNEL ISLANDS NATIONAL PARK

Santa Cruz Island

Port Hueneme

Santa Rosa Island

Anacapa Island

Six Flags Magic Mountain (1) & Hurricane Harbor (5)

(22 miles to NW of Downtown L.A.)
🚗 Fwy I-5 (Golden State), exit Valencia; Magic Mountain Parkway
🚆 Metrolink, station Santa Clarita, then bus 10 or 20

Knott's Berry Farm (2), Adventure City (4) & Movieland Wax Museum (15)

(40 miles to SE of Downtown L.A.)
🚗 Fwy I-405, Fwy I-5 (Santa Ana) or Fwy I-91, exit Beach Blvd
🚆 Metrolink station Fullerton
🚌 MTA 460

Disneyland (3)

(30 miles south of Downtown L.A.)
🚗 Fwy I-405 (San Diego) or I-5 (Santa Ana), exit Disneyland, Laguna Canyon Road (Hwy 133) west
🚌 Greyhound

Wild Rivers Waterpark (6)

(53 miles to SE of Downtown L.A.)
🚗 Fwy I-405 (San Diego), exit Irvine Center Drive

Santa Barbara (7–14)

(100 miles to N of Downtown L.A.)
🚗 Fwy US-101 (Ventura) or PCH-1, then Fwy US-101
🚆 Amtrak, station Santa Barbara
🚌 AMT 434

Crystal Cathedral (16) & Bowers Museum (17)

(41 miles to S-E of Downtown L.A.)
🚗 Fwy I-5 (Santa Ana), exit 17th Street at Santa Ana

San Nicolas Island

Orange County Museum of Art (18) & Balboa Island (19)

(50 miles to SE of Downtown L.A.)
🚗 Fwy I-405 (San Diego), exit Jamboree Road, (L) Santa Barbara Drive (L) San Clemente
🚆 Metrolink, station Newport Beach

Laguna Beach (20)

(60 miles to SE of Downtown L.A.)
🚗 Fwy I-405 (San Diego), exit Laguna Canyon Rd (Hwy 133) West

Irvine Museum (21)

(47 miles to SE of Downtown L.A.)
🚗 Fwy I-405 (San Diego), exit Jamboree Rd

Channel Islands (22)

Crossing between 1.30am and 3am
🚢 **Ventura Island Packers Company**
☎ 805/642-1393
1867 Spinnaker Dr.

🚢 **Santa Barbara Truth Aquatics**
☎ 805/962-1127
SEA Landing, 301 W. Cabrillo Blvd

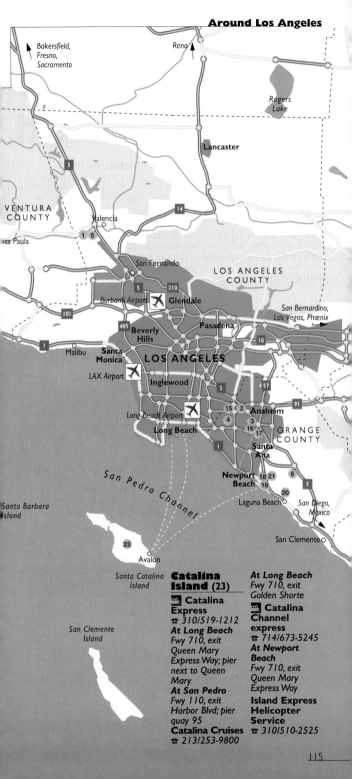

Bakersfield,
Fresno,
Sacramento

Reno

Rogers
Lake

Lancaster

VENTURA
COUNTY

Valencia

nta Paula

5

San Fernando

LOS ANGELES
COUNTY

Burbank Airport

Glendale

210

San Bernardino,
Las Vegas, Phœnix

101

Beverly
Hills

Pasadena

405

10

1

Santa
Monica

LOS ANGELES

Malibu

LAX Airport

Inglewood

15 2

Long Beach Airport

4

Anaheim

57

91

3

Long Beach

16

17

ORANGE
COUNTY

Santa
Ana

1

San Pedro Channel

Newport
Beach

18 21

19

6

Santa Barbara
Island

Laguna Beach

20

San Diego,
Mexico

San Clemente

23

Avalon

Santa Catalina
Island

San Clemente
Island

Catalina Island (23)

Catalina Express
☎ 310/519-1212
At Long Beach
Fwy 710, exit
Queen Mary
Express Way; pier
next to Queen
Mary
At San Pedro
Fwy 110, exit
Harbor Blvd; pier
quay 95
Catalina Cruises
☎ 213/253-9800

At Long Beach
Fwy 710, exit
Golden Shorte
Catalina Channel express
☎ 714/673-5245
At Newport Beach
Fwy 710, exit
Queen Mary
Express Way

Island Express Helicopter Service
☎ 310/510-2525

To remain young at heart, Californians simply invented theme parks for children… and for grown-ups. And the most famous of them all are concentrated in Los Angeles and Orange County. From a day with Mickey Mouse to the vertiginous rollercoasters of Six Flags Magic Mountain, there is something for all tastes and all ages.

Further afield

Six Flags Magic Mountain (1)
26101 Magic Mountain Pkwy, Valencia, CA 91355 ☎ 818/367-5695

🅿 ⬛ 🕐 *Memorial Day–Labor Day: Mon.–Thu., Sun. 10am–10pm; Fri.–Sat. 10am–midnight/Labor Day–Memorial Day: Sat., Sun., school vacations 10am–8pm* ● *$39; children under 4 ft, over-60s $19.50* 🏬 💻 ⊞

The ultimate park for rollercoaster enthusiasts. Rides include the world's tallest and fastest stand-up rollercoaster and the world's largest looping rollercoaster. In spring 2000, Goliath opened, the first giant thrill ride of the new millennium. The park's ten themed areas also feature a float on Roaring Rapids and a nature walk through The High Sierra Territory.

Knott's Berry Farm (2)
8039 Beach Boulevard, Buena Park, CA 90620 ☎ 714/827-1776

(between La Palma Ave and Crescent St.) 🅿 ⬛ 🕐 *June–Sep. 15: daily 9am–midnight/Sep. 15–May: Mon.–Fri. 10am–6pm; Sat. 10am–10pm; Sun. 10am–7pm/closed Dec. 25* ● *$38; children, over-65s $28; after 4pm $16.95* 🏬 💻 ⊞

The nation's first theme park, which began as a berry stand in 1920 and later expanded to include a ghost town attraction in 1940, now features more than 165 rides, shows, attractions, restaurants and shops. Themed areas include Camp Snoopy, Old West Ghost Town, Fiesta Village, The Boardwalk, Indian Trails and Wild Water Wilderness. GhostRider and Supreme Scream are two of the park's most popular rollercoaster rides.

Disneyland (3)
1313 Harbor Boulevard, Anaheim, CA 90802 ☎ 714/781-4565

🅿 ⬛ 🕐 *June–Sep. 15: Sun.–Fri. 8am–1am; Sat. 9am–1am/Sep. 15–May: Mon.–Fri. 10am–6pm; Sat. 9am–midnight; Sun. 9am–10pm* ● *$41; under-9s $31; over-60s $39/2-day passport $76; 5-day passport $99* 🏬 💻 ⊞

Touted as 'The Happiest Place On Earth', the world's most famous theme park originated in Southern California 45 years ago. Constantly improving what seems already to be the perfect paradise of family fun, the park includes eight themed areas: Adventureland, featuring the Indiana Jones Adventure; Critter Country, a backwoods setting for Splash Mountain; Fantasyland, a storybook kingdom; Frontierland, a return to the Old West; Main Street, U.S.A.; New Orleans Square, with the Haunted Mansion; Mickey's Toontown; and the futuristic Tomorrowland.

Not forgetting

■ **Hobby & Adventure City (4)** 1238 S. Beach Blvd, Anaheim, CA 90680 ☎ 714/236-9300 *Merry-go-rounds, shows and amusements aimed at small children.*

■ **Hurricane Harbor (5)** 2060 Magic Mountain Pkwy, Valencia, CA 91355 ☎ 818/367-5965 *A pirate theme park featuring dozens of water attractions for the entire family.*

■ **Wild Rivers Waterpark (6)** 8770 Irvine Center Dr., Irvine, CA 92618 ☎ 949/768-9453 *There are 40 water rides and other attractions in this lush setting.*

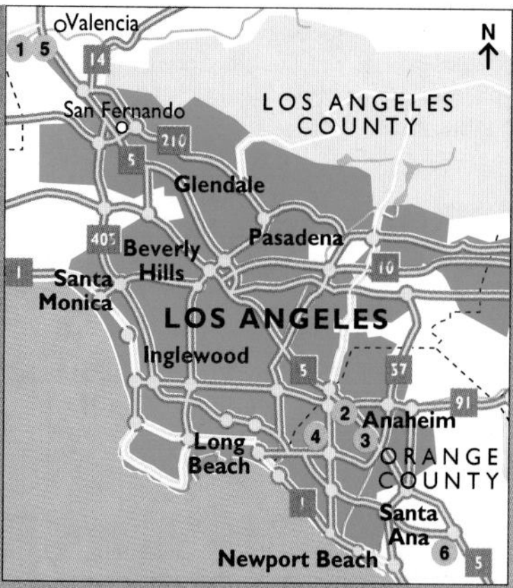
Valencia
1 5
14
San Fernando
210
5
LOS ANGELES COUNTY
Glendale
405
Beverly Hills
Pasadena
1
Santa Monica
10
LOS ANGELES
Inglewood
5
57
2 Anaheim
3
4
91
Long Beach
ORANGE COUNTY
1
Santa Ana
Newport Beach
6
5
N

GOTHAM CITY
BACKLOT
1

3

2

3

One of the best ways to reach Santa Barbara, a place especially favored by Angelinos wanting to get away from it all, is along a picturesque coastal route, the Pacific Coast Highway. The architecture of this elegant and modest seaside locality, and its numerous streets with their Spanish names, recall its Hispanic heritage.

Further afield

Santa Barbara Botanic Garden (7)
1212 Mission Canyon Dr., Santa Barbara, CA 93101 ☎ 805/682-4726

🅿 🔲 🕐 *Mon.–Fri. 9am–4pm; Sat., Sun. 9am–5pm* ● *$3; under-12s $1; under-17s, over-60s $2* 🔲 *Mon.–Wed., Fri. 2pm; Thu., Sat., Sun. 10.30am, 2pm* 🔲

In 1926, in order not to see one of the most beautiful canyons in the region transformed into a residential area, Anna Blaksley Bliss declared it a botanical nature reserve. Today its 65 acres and five miles of footpaths offer a superb setting for the study of Californian flora, of which 1,000 species are rare or indigenous.

Mission Santa Barbara (8)
2201 Laguna Street, Santa Barbara, CA 93101 ☎ 805/682-4713

🅿 🔲 🕐 *daily 9am–5pm* ● *$3; under-16s free* 🔲

Founded in 1786, this 'Queen of Missions' is the only one of 21 missions built in California by the Franciscans still in operation, and the best preserved. Visit its gardens, its museum comprising living quarters full of period pieces, and the church with its twin towers.

Santa Barbara Museum of Art (9)
1130 State Street, Santa Barbara, CA 93101 ☎ 805/963-4364

🕐 *Tue.–Thu., Sat. 11am–5pm; Fri. 11am–9pm; Sun. noon–5pm* ● *$5; over-62s $3; under-17s $2; under-6s free/free on Thursdays* 🔲 🔲

An exceptional regional museum including a permanent collection of 19th-century Impressionists highlighting Monet, Chagall and Matisse as well as the works of O'Keeffe, Hooper and Eakins. Don't miss Monet's *Villa at Bordighera* or the Lansdowne marble sculpture of *Hermes*. Also features Greek and Roman antiquities, a major photographic collection, 20th-century and contemporary works and impressive traveling exhibitions.

County Courthouse (10)
1100 Anacapa Street, Santa Barbara, CA 93101 ☎ 805/962-6464

🕐 *Mon.–Fri. 8am–5pm; Sat., Sun. 9am–5pm* ● *free* 🔲 *Mon.–Sat. 2pm* 🔲

The interiors of this castle-like, Spanish-Moorish courthouse, built in 1929, feature hand-carved wooden doors and archways, Tunisian tile mosaics and colorful murals, including one depicting the history of the county. The tower provides exceptional views.

Not forgetting

■ **Santa Barbara Historical Museum (11)** 136 E. De la Guerra St., Santa Barbara, CA 93101 ☎ 805/966-1601 *Old toys, period costumes, mementos and documents recounting Santa Barbara's past.* ■ **El Presidio (12)** 123 E. Canon Perdido St., Santa Barbara, CA 93101 ☎ 805/966-9719 *Built in 1782, El Cuartel is all that remains of the four Royal Spanish military outposts built in Alta.* ■ **Santa Barbara Winery (13)** 202 Anacapa St., Santa Barbara, CA 93101 ☎ 805/963-3646 *The oldest winery in the country set up in 1962. Guided tour and wine tasting.* ■ **Maritime Museum (14)** Harbor Way, Santa Barbara, CA 93109 ☎ 805/962-8404 *Discover the maritime heritage of the Santa Barbara Channel and central coast of California which began thousands of years ago with the Chumash indigenous people who were seafarers and fishermen. Fascinating interactive activities and artifacts included.*

Orange County, now unfortunately almost totally without orange groves, is renowned for its luxury beach resorts, its museums, its various types of amusement park ➡ 116 and its artists' colonies. It is said to be so conservative that only right-hand turns are allowed…

Further afield

Movieland Wax Museum (15)
7711 Beach Boulevard, Buena Park, CA 90620 ☎ 714/522-1154

(La Palma Ave) 🅿 ⬜ 🕐 *Mon.–Fri. 10am–6pm; Sat., Sun. 9am–7pm* ● *$12.95; under-12s $6.95; over-65s $10.95*

Some 300 waxworks here immortalize over 75 years of American cinema. Stars of the big screen but also of politics, sport and the media, dressed in original costumes donated by the people depicted, are placed in authentic settings inspired by *Gone with the Wind* or *The Wizard of Oz*. Gloria Estefan, John Travolta, Jack Nicholson and the *Star Trek* team are among the latest creations.

Crystal Cathedral (16)
12141 Lewis Street, Garden Grove, CA 92840 ☎ 714/971-4013

(Chapman Ave) 🅿 🕐 *Mon.–Sat. 9am–5pm;* **services** *Sun. 9.30am, 11am* 🍴 *Mon.–Sat. 9am–4pm* ● *$2; under-12s free* **Pageants** ● *$20–30* 🎟

This 11-story high architectural feat in the form of a four-pointed star made from steel tubing on which rest 10,000 sheets of glass, is the work of Philip Johnson. The domain of the well-publicized evangelist Robert Schuller, the main annual events are two pageants held on the appropriate dates: *The Glory of Christmas* and *The Glory of Easter*.

Bowers Museum (17)
2002 N. Main Street, Santa Ana, CA 92706 ☎ 714/567-3600

(I–5) 🅿 🕐 *Tue., Wed., Fri.–Sun. 10am–4pm; Thu. 10am–7pm* ● *$6*

The largest museum in Orange County boasts more than 83,000 items, and specializes in the preservation and display of pre-Columbian, African and Oceanian art, and that of the American Indians. The presentation allows you to compare these different cultures throughout the ages.

Orange County Museum of Art (18)
850 San Clemente Dr., Newport Beach, CA 92606 ☎ 949/759-1122

(Jamboree Rd and Santa Barbara Dr.) 🅿 🍴 🕐 *Tue.–Sun. 11am–5pm* ● *$5; under-16s free; students, over-62s $4; free on Tuesdays* 🎟 🏛

Focusing on the art and artists of California, the exhibits range from Impressionist paintings to provocative contemporary works.

Not forgetting

■ **Balboa Island & Peninsula (19)** PCH 1, Newport Beach *Surrounded by protected beaches, visitors experience the tranquility of life in the slow lane as they walk the boardwalk and explore this sophisticated beach community. Whale watching, sport fishing and sightseeing boats available; the Balboa Pavilion, once a Victorian boathouse, is where trips to Catalina Island, whale watching and sightseeing boats start from.* ■ **Laguna Beach (20)** *The twisting streets of this beach resort surrounded by jagged cliffs are packed with galleries, stores and cafes. This artists' colony welcomes every year the Pageant of the Masters, a live representation of famous paintings and statues, and the Sawdust Festival, a meeting place for musicians, mime artists and artisans to show off their work.* ■ **Irvine Museum (21)** 18881 Von Karman Ave, 11th floor, Irvine, CA 92805 ☎ 949/476-2565 *The museum of Californian Impressionists (1890-1930). The works were collected by the granddaughter of James Irvine, Joan.*

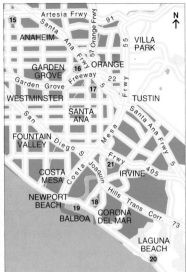

A boat ride to a Southern California island provides not only a pleasant excursion at sea, but a choice of several island destinations. Visit Catalina, originally the 'kingdom' of chewing gum magnate William Wrigley Jr., and also a favorite haunt of eminent author, Zane Grey. Or opt for a nature adventure at the Channel Islands National Park.

Further afield

Channel Islands (22)
Channel Islands National Park Visitor Center,
1901 Spinnaker Drive, Ventura, VE 90000 ☎ 805/658-5730

Whale watching 🕐 *June–Oct. information Channel Islands National Marine Sanctuary* ☎ *805/966-7107 Camping (reservations essential) Biospherics* ☎ *800/365-2267* ● *$2.50* 📷

Located 12–50 miles offshore, the Channel Islands are without a doubt one of the most beautiful nature reserves in California. They were inhabited by the Chumash Indians, 'Island people', until 1542 and the arrival of the explorer Juan Rodríguez. In the 18th and 19th centuries, the archipelago was exploited for hunting, fur trapping, and cattle and sheep farming, to the point where the natural resources were endangered. It was not until 1980 that five of these islands – Santa Barbara, Anacapa, Santa Cruz, San Miguel and Santa Rosa – were made into a national park, and not until 1988 that the Nature Conservancy started to manage a portion of Santa Cruz island. Today, the islands are home to a wide variety of animal and plant species, of which 145 are native. You can learn to recognize them thanks to trips organized by the Rangers. All the islands differ from each other, both in their morphology and in the diversity of their occupiers. On the three small islands of Anacapa you will find, for example, Chumash archeological sites and the Anacapa deer mouse. On Santa Rosa, the furthermost island of the archipelago, you will see the fossil of a dwarf mammoth discovered in 1994, Torrey pines and Vail & Vickers, the only working ranch (until 2002). As for the sea, the range of possible activities is just as wide: you can dive, kayak, fish and watch blue and hump-back whales. If you decide to stay for a few days, you can really play at being Robinson Crusoe as there are no mod cons: no water, no electricity, no restaurants, no hotels … and no flushing toilets!

Catalina Island (23)

Wrigley Memorial & Botanical Garden Avalon Canyon Rd 🕐 *daily 8am–5pm* ● *$3* ☎ *310/510-2288 Casino* / *Casino Way* 🕐 *guided tours daily* ● *$8.50* ☎ *310/510-8687 Catalina Island Museum* / *Casino Way* 🕐 *Easter–Jan: daily 10.30am–4pm/Jan.–Easter: Fri.–Wed. 10.30.–4pm* ☎ *310/510-2414*

Twenty-two miles across the sea, Catalina Island offers a plethora of activities for the outdoor enthusiast including horseback riding, golf, snorkeling, ocean rafting, camping, boating, para-sailing, scuba diving, bicycling, kayaking, nature tours and glass-bottom boats. The nearly 40-acre Wrigley Botanical Garden has plants from around the world with special emphasis on Catalina native plants, many of which are extremely rare. An education and display center includes a film on the garden. The landmark circular, red-tiled Art-Deco Casino (not a gambling hall, but a ballroom) was completed in May 1929, and houses a functioning movie theater and museum which focuses on the cultural history of the island, with special exhibits on the history of the steamship, island pottery and tiles and archeological objects. Guided tours of the casino are offered by Discovery Tours; the quaint village includes shops, restaurants and hotels.

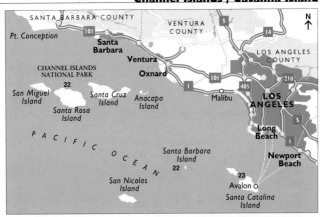

123

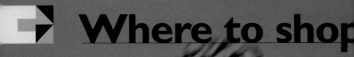

Taxes
In Los Angeles, the tax on all articles
(apart from food) is 8.25%. For large
purchases, ask in the store if they
offer tax-free shopping.

Where to shop

Sizes: Shoes

US		UK
5½	=	4
6½	=	5
7½	=	6
8½	=	7
9½	=	8
10½	=	9

Sizes: Women's clothes

US		UK
12	=	10
14	=	12
16	=	14

Farmers' Markets
Los Angeles is renowned for
its small organic markets, held
in all districts of the city.
Hollywood *Ivar Ave (Sunset Blvd)*
🕐 *Sun. 8.30am-1pm*
Santa Monica *Arizona Blvd*
🕐 *Wed. 9.30am-2pm;*
Sat. 8.30am-1pm
Venice *Venice Blvd and Venice Wy*
🕐 *Fri. 7am-11am*
West Hollywood *Plummer Park,*
7377 Santa Monica Blvd
🕐 *Mon. 9am-2pm*
The most tourist-oriented
Farmers' Market houses 150
booths and restaurants under
its roof ➡ 52
6333 W. 3rd St. (Fairfax Blvd)
🕐 *Mon.-Sat. 9am-8pm;*
Sun. 10am-5pm

Parking

The shopping malls often have their own free parking lots; in towns such as Santa Monica and Beverly Hills, take advantage of two hours without charge in public parking lots. At exclusive stores, someone will park your car for you.

68
Stores

Trader Joe's

Southern California would not be the same without this incredible discount supermarket. The products offer excellent value for money, as well as excellent special offers. There are numerous stores in L.A., including: 3212 Pico Blvd (between 32nd and 33rd Sts), Santa Monica ☎ *310/581-0253*

INDEX BY TYPE

The first malls in Los Angeles opened in the 1930s and reflected the expansion of suburbia and the beginning of the motor car boom. Nowadays, there are almost a hundred of these meccas for the consumer, with stores both large and small, restaurants, movie theaters and, of course, innumerable parking lots.

Where to shop

Universal City Walk (1)

Universal City Dr., Studio City, CA 91608
☎ 818/622-4455
(Lankershim Blvd)
🅿 **Shopping mall**
⬛ 🕙 *Mon.–Thu.*
11am–9pm;
Fri., Sat.
11am–11pm 🎏
⬛

A stone's throw from the Universal Studios main entrance ➡ 96, this pedestrian-only strip is a fantasy environment famous for its carnival-like streetlife and wacky storefronts. Among the eye-poppers are a pink Chevy crashing through a freeway sign and a gigantic gorilla framing a store entrance. Some shops are worth a detour: the Nature Company specializing in environmentally sensitive products or Things From Another World which has science-fiction memorabilia.

Beverly Center (2)

8500 Beverly Dr., Los Angeles, CA 90048
☎ 310/854-0070
(La Cienaga Blvd)
🅿 **Shopping mall**
⬛ 🕙 *Mon.–Fri.*
10am–9pm;
Sat. 10am–8pm;
Sun. 11am–6pm
🎏 ⬛

With its angular lines and its steel-gray, windowless façade, the Beverly Center looks like a giant spaceship. Celebrities often come here to shop at the extremely varied range of stores: male ready-to-wear at Hugo Boss, cosmetics at MAC, shoes at Charles David, etc. You can also change your look and your hairstyle at Carlton Hair International, buy half-price tickets for shows at Times Tix, haunt the shelves at Macy's, and take a break at the Hard Rock Cafe.

Century City Center (3)

10250 Santa Monica Boulevard, Los Angeles, CA 90067
☎ 310/553-5300
(Ave of the Stars)
🅿 **Shopping mall**
⬛ 🕙 *Mon.–Fri.*
10am–9pm;
Sat., Sun.
10am–6pm 🎏 ⬛

The only outdoor shopping mall in L.A. is set on Twentieth Century Fox's former backlot. Numerous luxury stores jostle for the attention and the wallet of even the most difficult-to-please visitor. You will find very popular chains such as Crate & Barrel ➡ 130 and

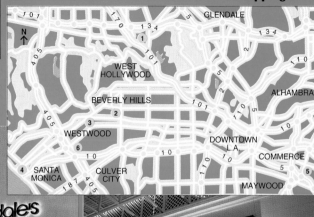

3

Ann Taylor, but also Brentano's bookshop, Bloomingdale's and Macy's department stores. Finish off your day by seeing a movie in the 14-screen theater complex.

Santa Monica Place (4)

395 Santa Monica Pl., Santa Monica, CA 90067
☎ *310/553-5300 (between 2nd and 4th Sts)* **P**
Shopping mall 🗖
🕒 *Mon.–Sat. 10am–9pm; Sun. 11am–6pm* 🎬 **□**
Architect Frank Gehry designed this whimsical-looking three-story mall with its

excellent cross-section of stores. There is Brookstone for inventive home, office and travel gadgets, or Frederick's of Hollywood
➥ 132 for lingerie; The Store of Knowledge is a winner with its educational yet fun toys, while the Bombay Company has reasonable colonial-style furnishings. For more selection there are department stores, Robinsons-May and Macy's. And for food, Eatz's with quality and selection is second to none in L.A.

Citadel Factory Store (5)

5675 E. Telegraph Road, City of Commerce, CA 90040
☎ *323/888-1220 (I–5 then Atlantic Blvd exit)*
P **Shopping mall**
🗖 🕒 *Mon.–Sat. 10am–8pm; Sun. 10am–6pm* 🎬 **□**
The only factory outlet in the city is located in an old tire factory complete with crenelated walls, bas-reliefs and giant guardian griffins modeled after a 7th-century Assyrian palace. Inside you will find brands such as Ann Taylor, Eddie Bauer, London

Fog, Vans Shoes, Betsey Johnson and Samsonite, sold at prices 30–70% less than in retail stores.

Westside Pavilion (6)

10830 W. Pico Blvd, West Los Angeles, CA 90064
☎ *310/474-6255 (Westwood Blvd)*
P **Shopping mall**
🗖 🕒 *Mon.–Fri. 10am–9pm; Sat. 10am–8pm; Sun. 11am–6pm* 🎬 **□**
An elegant mall where you shop in an atrium lit by a glass wall behind a colored façade. Home base of Nordstrom and Robinsons-May.

In the area

 Where to stay: ➡ 16
Where to eat: ➡ 38 ➡ 40
After dark: ➡ 74
What to see: ➡ 86 ➡ 88 ➡ 90

➡ Where to shop

San Antonio Winery (7)
737 Lamar Street, Los Angeles, CA 90000 ☎ 323/223-1401

(Cardinal St.) 🅿 *Wines* ▢ 🕒 *Sun.–Tue. 10am–6pm; Wed.–Sat. 10am–7pm* ▦

San Antonio Winery is the last bastion of winemaking in a region which – incredible but true – was formerly covered with vineyards. The grapes of this wine grower, in existence since 1917, are now cultivated in Central California, but the wines, often excellent, are still produced here. In addition, the establishment features a wine-tasting room, a free personal guided tour and an authentic Italian restaurant.

Grand Central Market (8)
317 Broadway, Los Angeles, CA 90014 ☎ 213/624-2378

(between 7th and 8th Sts) **Food market** 🗒 🕒 *daily 9am–6pm*

An L.A. institution since 1917, this bustling indoor bazaar is a visual – and culinary – treat. Wander the aisles past piles of artfully stacked oranges, tomatoes, peppers as well as ethnic varieties like tomatillos and plantains. The meat counters offer everything from the familiar to animal parts you may not have known existed. You can also stock up on exotic spices, a wide array of legumes or Chinese herbal concoctions. For a perfect finish, sidle up to the counter at any of the eateries for a budget bite. Favorites include fish tacos at Maria's Pescado Frito and steamy soup at the China Cafe.

La Plata Cigar Company (9)
1026 Grand Avenue, Los Angeles, CA 90015 ☎ 213/747-8561

(between 7th and 8th Sts) **Cigar maker** ▢ 🕒 *Mon.–Fri. 8am–4pm*

The Cuban cigar rollers at La Plata have been churning out stogies for more than 50 years. If you visit the only remaining handmade cigar factory in L.A., the friendly staff is likely to invite you to the back room to observe their craftsmen at work. True aficionados, though, may prefer to stock up for their favorite vice inside La Plata's grand humidor.

Santee Alley (10)
(Between Olympic Blvd and 12th St.) Market 🕒 daily 10am–6pm

This pedestrianized strip in the Garment District has the feel of a Middle Eastern bazaar. Come here to pick up designer knockoffs at good prices, but for true bargains be prepared to haggle.

Not forgetting

◼ **L.A. Flower Market (11)** 754 Wall Street, Los Angeles, CA 90014 ☎ 213/622-1966 *This symphony of color and aromas has been around since 1913 and, until a couple of years ago, was primarily a wholesale market. With recently expanded hours and rock-bottom prices, anyone can now wander the halls and stock up on armloads of Hawaiian ginger or lilies.*
◼ **Cooper Building (12)** 860 S. Los Angeles St., Los Angeles, CA 90014 ☎ 213/622-1139 *The epicenter of L.A.'s Garment District, the Cooper Building has two floors of heavily discounted fashions by L.A. and international designers, including samples for men, women and children, plus accessories and shoes.*

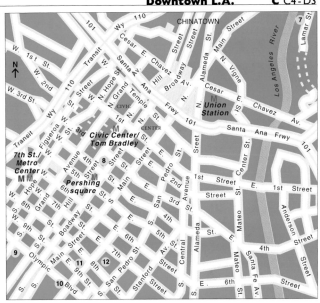

7

Downtown, where L.A. began over two centuries ago, is one of the most fascinating neighborhoods. Join a Saturday morning walking tour ($5) with the nonprofit L.A. Conservancy (tel. 213-623-2489).

10

8

129

Where to shop

Crate & Barrel (13)
75 W. Colorado Boulevard, Pasadena, CA 91105 ☎ 626/683-8000

(Leonard J. Pieroni St.) **Articles for the home** ▢ ◯ *Mon.–Sat. 10am–9pm; Sun. 11am–6pm* Century Shopping Center ➡ 126

The ideal spot to find articles for the house, the kitchen and the bathroom. The style is classic, making the products as suitable for daily use as for special occasions. Prices remain very reasonable.

Canyon Beachwear (14)
34 Hugus Alley, Pasadena, CA 91105 ☎ 626/564-0752

(Colorado Blvd) **Swimming costumes, accessories** ▢ ◯ *Mon.–Sat. 10am–9pm; Sun. 11am–6pm* Beverly Center ➡ 126; 2937 Main St., Santa Monica

This store stands out for its great selection and friendly service. All styles are represented, from the flamboyant *Baywatch*-type one-piece to the tankini to the barely visible string. You can mix sizes or find a swimsuit with a short skirt if you have a less-than-perfect figure; nothing is too much trouble for the friendly staff who will find you the ideal suit to hide those extra pounds.

Del Mano Gallery (15)
33 E. Colorado Boulevard, Pasadena, CA 91105 ☎ 626/793-6648

(Fair Oaks Ave) **Art gallery** ▢ ◯ *Mon.–Thu. 10am–6pm; Fri., Sat. 10am–9pm; Sun. 11am–6pm* 11981 San Vincente Blvd, Los Angeles ☎ 310/476-8508

This handsome gallery is well known for its sophisticated array of fine arts and crafts by American artists. Let yourself be tempted by ceramics, lamps, glass, jewelry, furniture, and handpainted silks, all original designs and handmade. Tags identify the artists and provide a synopsis of their career and philosophy.

Distant Lands (16)
56 S. Raymond Avenue, Pasadena, CA 91105 ☎ 626/449-3220

(E. Colorado Blvd) **Travel bookshop** ▢ ◯ *Mon.–Thu. 10.30am–6pm; Fri., Sat. 10.30am–9pm; Sun. 11am–6pm* @ distantland@deltanat.com

Need ideas for your next trip? Stop in at Distant Lands whose floor-to-ceiling shelves are jam-packed with guidebooks, gorgeously photographed coffee-table books and language books. Travel accessories from water filters to plug adaptors fill an entire section, and the knowledgeable staff will make every effort to help you find just what you need.

Not forgetting

■ **CP Shades (17)** 20 S. Raymond Avenue, Pasadena, CA 91105 ☎ 626/564-9304 *Beautifully designed clothing made in Sausalito in linen, cotton and silk and hand-dyed in rich monochromatic colors.* ■ **Sur la Table (18)** 161 W. Colorado Blvd, Pasadena, CA 91105 ☎ 626/744-9987 *Whether you are an amateur cook or a real chef, this is where you will find all the utensils to make the ideal souffle or sushi.* ■ **Urban Outfitters (19)** 139 W. Colorado Blvd, Pasadena, CA 91105 ☎ 626/449-1818 *Hip warehouse-type store with young designer clothing and fun furnishings from around the world; also in Santa Monica.*

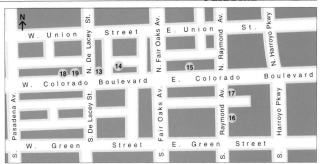

Colorado Boulevard is the main artery of Old Town Pasadena, the city's historic district. In the early 1990s, the area underwent a major face-lift and has since evolved into a hugely popular place for strolling, dining, people watching and, yes, shopping.

In the area

➡ **Where to stay:** ➡ 20
➡ **Where to eat:** ➡ 44
➡ **After dark:** ➡ 68 ➡ 70 ➡ 74 ➡ 76 ➡ 78 ➡ 80
➡ **What to see:** ➡ 86 ➡ 96 ➡ 98

➡ Where to shop

Samuel French Theater & Film Bookshop (20)
7623 Sunset Blvd, Los Angeles, CA 90028 ☎ 323/876-0570

(N. Martel Ave) **Bookshop** ▢ ◷ *Mon.–Fri. 10am–6pm; Sat. 10am–5pm*
▥ *11963 Ventura Blvd, Studio City* ☎ *818/762-0535*

Need a script of *Gone with the Wind* or the musical score to *Oklahoma?*
You'll find them both at Samuel French, L.A.'s quintessential one-stop-
shopping source for any screenplay or theater script ever printed.
Budding Steven Spielbergs might also want to scan through their all-
encompassing selection of books on cinematography, directing,
animation, special effects and other filmic subjects.

Hollywood Toys & Costumes (21)
6600 Hollywood Boulevard, Los Angeles, CA 90028 ☎ 323/464-4444

(Whitley Ave) **Toys, costumes** ▢ ◷ *Mon.–Fri. 9am–9pm; Sat. 10am–7pm;*
Sun. 10.30am–5pm

Hollywood prop masters and Halloween fans are among those who have
made the pilgrimage to this sprawling empire of imagination for nearly
half a century. Look out for the sunken monster pit beneath the glass
floor as you enter, then browse through a huge inventory of masks, wigs,
make-up, tombstones and gargoyles and just about every costume you
can imagine.

Playmates (22)
6438 Hollywood Boulevard, Hollywood, CA 90028 ☎ 323/464-7636

(Wilcox Ave) **Lingerie** ▢ ◷ *daily 10am–8pm*

As soon as you walk past the provocative shop windows, you know you're
in for a bit of a naughty adventure. This store is, after all, where
professional strippers get their vinyl teddies and kinky heels. Non-pros and
those with tamer tastes can pick through a great collection of ingenious
swimwear and lacy lingerie. Don't leave without checking out the famous
You are a Star mural which graces the Wilcox Ave side of the store.

Panpipes Magickal Marketplace (23)
1641 Cahuenga Boulevard, Hollywood, CA 90028 ☎ 323/462-7078

(Selma Ave) **Esotericism** ▢ ◷ *daily 11am–7pm*

The nation's oldest occult supply store is a well-known destination in the
pagan community, which it has served since 1961. Pick from a huge
selection of oils, herbs, potions and other ingredients at these crammed
headquarters of mysticism. The skilled staff will whip up a custom-blend,
designed to cure any ailment real or imagined; also the place to stock up
on crystal balls, cauldrons and ouija boards.

Not forgetting

■ **Heaven 27 (24)** *6316 Yucca St., Hollywood, CA 90028* ☎ *323/871-9044*
This boutique belonging to Sofia Coppola, daughter of Francis Ford, distributes her
range of Milkfed clothing, much sought-after by Hollywood trendsetters.
■ **Frederick's of Hollywood (25)** *6608 Hollywood Blvd, Hollywood,*
CA 90028 ☎ *323/466-8506 The wildest and most kitsch range of ladies' lingerie,*
complemented by a museum of underwear worn by the stars for films or shows.

25

Major efforts are underway to restore glamor and glory to Glittertown. Old visitor favorites like the Hollywood Walk of Fame and Mann's Chinese Theater will soon be joined by a new entertainment complex scheduled to bring Oscar back to Hollywood Boulevard for the annual Academy Awards extravaganza.

21

24

24

Though you're not likely to run into your favorite celebrities in the flesh, you can increase the odds: go to the latest hotspots in dining, drinking and dancing; get tickets to a studio taping; or pick up a shoot sheet, from the Film Permit Office in Hollywood. Or, if all else fails, check out any of the stores below to at least catch a twinge of that Hollywood vibe.

 # Where to shop

It's a Wrap (26)
3315 W. Magnolia Avenue, Burbank, CA 91505 ☎ 818/567-7366

(N. California St.) **Secondhand clothes** ▣ ◐ *Mon.–Fri. 11am–8pm; Sat., Sun. 11am–6pm*

Clothing worn during filming for TV or the big screen usually ends up in the studio's wardrobe department to be reused for future productions. When it doesn't, it goes to It's a Wrap for resale to the public. All Hollywood hand-me-downs have been cleaned and sport coded tags identifying the show or movie they're originally from, including some big hits like *American Beauty, As Good as it Gets* and *Charmed*. Prices are 30-90% off retail; it's possible to get a simple T-shirt from *Beverly Hills 90210* for just $15. If, however, the threads have touched the skin of Sharon Stone, Jack Nicholson or other A-list celebs, expect to pay premium prices: these are considered collectors' items.

Larry Edmunds (27)
6644 Hollywood Boulevard, Hollywood, CA 90028 ☎ 323/463-3273

(Whitley Ave) **Bookshop, accessories, curios** ▣ ◐ *Mon.–Sat. 10am–6pm*

Trawling through this fascinating store filled with Hollywood scripts, posters, movie stills, old magazines and lots of other stuff could easily take the better part of an afternoon. It also claims to have the largest collection of books about movies and the theater.

The Place & Co (28)
8820 S. Sepulveda Boulevard, Westchester, CA 90045 ☎ 310/645-1539

(La Tijera Ave) **Secondhand clothes** ▣ ◐ *Mon.–Sat. 10am–6pm*

In business for 36 years, this boutique sells barely worn haute couture at bargain prices. Shall we drop some names? How about Hugo Boss, Armani, Oscar de la Renta, Helmut Lang…? Everything for sale was once owned by a celebrity but, alas, their identity remains a secret. Discretion is key here.

Moletown (29)
900 La Brea, Hollywood, CA 90038 ☎ 323/851-01111

(Santa Monica Blvd and Melrose Ave) **Accessories** ▣ ◐ *Mon.–Fri. 10am–6pm; Sat. 11am–5pm*

All items in Moletown – from hats to jackets and T-shirts and not forgetting coffee mugs – are embellished with photos or logos from TV programs, sitcoms or contemporary films, such as *Pokémon* or great classics such as *The Wizard of Oz* or *Indiana Jones*.

Not forgetting
■ **Warner Bros Studios Store (30)** 4000 Warner Blvd, Burbank, CA 91522 ☎ 818/954-2550 *Items stamped with the Warner logo or decorated with a cartoon character can be found on sale in this store next to the studio* ➡ 96. ■ **Reel Clothes & Props (31)** 12132 Ventura Blvd, Studio City, CA 91602 ☎ 818/508-7762 *Similar to It's a Wrap but more crammed; labels only identify the studio but not the show. For collectibles, check their website at www.reelclothes.com.* ■ **Paramount Pictures Store (32)** 5555 Melrose Ave, Los Angeles, CA 90036 ☎ 323/956-3036 *A store to be recommended especially to fans of Star Trek, filmed here at Paramount* ➡ 96.

In the area
- ▶ **Where to stay:** ➥ 20 ➥ 22
- ▶ **Where to eat:** ➥ 46 ➥ 48
- ▶ **After dark:** ➥ 68 ➥ 72 ➥ 74 ➥ 76 ➥ 78 ➥ 82
- ▶ **What to see:** ➥ 136

Where to shop

Bodhi Tree (34)
8585 Melrose Avenue, West Hollywood, CA 90069 ☎ 310/659-1733

(Westbourne Dr.) **Bookshop** ◻ 🕐 *daily 10am–11pm/secondhand daily 10am–7pm*

The ultimate esoteric bookstore with departments from Inner Healing to UFOs, plus crystals, incense, oils and other New Age accoutrements; psychic readings and used bookstore in back.

Elixir Tonics & Teas (35)
8612 Melrose Avenue, West Los Angeles, CA 90046 ☎ 310/657-9300

(Huntley Ave) **Teas, infusions** ◻ 🕐 *Mon.–Fri. 10am–8pm; Sat. 10am–6pm; Sun. 11am–6pm* 🔲 🔲

Elixir is an oasis of calm and tranquility. Co-founders Jeffrey Stein and Edgar Veytia promise a total commitment to health and well-being, a philosophy that has resonated with Sharon Stone, Marisa Tomei and lots of other silver screen-stars. Only top-grade ingredients make up their unique blends of teas and tonics especially formulated by Elixir's trained herbalists.

Soolip Paperie & Soolip Bungalow (36)
8646 Melrose Avenue, West Hollywood, CA 90046 ☎ 310/360-1512

(Robertson Blvd) **Articles for the home, stationery** ◻ 🕐 *Mon.–Sat. 11am–7pm; Sun. noon–5pm*

You can find the gift for a friend who has already got it all at Soolip, an inspiring emporium of good taste housed in a rambling cluster of wooden cottages. For handmade wrapping paper, witty notecards and scented ink, browse through the Paperie, then visit the Bungalow for sumptuous bed and bath accessories and exquisite home furnishings.

Hustler Hollywood (37)
8920 Sunset Blvd, West Hollywood, CA 90046 ☎ 310/860-9009

🕐 *daily 10am–2pm* 🔲 *8am–2am*

The daughter of Larry Flint, the leading world pornographer, manages this store filled with lingerie, erotic accessories, videos and literature for all tastes, from the sophisticated to the sordid.

Tower Records (38)
8801 Sunset Blvd, West Hollywood ☎ 310/657-7300

🕐 *daily 9am–midnight* 🔢 *8844 Sunset Blvd, West Hollywood* 🕐 *daily 10am–10pm*

This legendary store stocks over 100,000 CDs and has an annex dedicated to classical music at 8844 Sunset Blvd.

Not forgetting

■ **Lemon Tree bungalow (39)** 8727 Santa Monica Blvd, West Hollywood, CA 90046 ☎ 310/657-0211 *This cute cottage is jam-packed with home accessories and gift items selected with personal style by owner Michelle Whang.*

West Hollywood is a haven of hipness and hedonism. Bisected by the Sunset Strip with legendary nightclubs ➔ 72 like the Roxy, Whisky and Viper Room, it is also home to L.A.'s cutting-edge creative design community headquartered at the Pacific Design Center and the heart of the city's gay and lesbian scene.

In the area
- **Where to stay:** ➡ 22 ➡ 24
- **Where to eat:** ➡ 44 ➡ 46 ➡ 48 ➡ 50 ➡ 52
- **After dark:** ➡ 68 ➡ 72 ➡ 74 ➡ 76 ➡ 78 ➡ 82
- **What to see:** ➡ 86 ➡ 96 ➡ 98 ➡ 100

➡ Where to shop

Jet Rag (40)
825 N. La Brea, Los Angeles, CA 90036 ☎ 323/393-0528

Secondhand clothes 🕐 *Mon.–Sat. 11.30–8pm; Sun. 11am–7.30pm* 🚹 **Slow**
7474 Melrose Ave, Los Angeles ☎ 323/655-3725

The first things you'll notice about Jet Rag are the faux missiles propping up the facade and the animal-skeleton mannequins propping up the clothes. Inside this lofty warehouse you'll find rack upon rack of mostly post-WWII American clothing in good condition. Their $1 sales on Thursday and Sunday are legendary among fashion vultures.

Jon Valdi (41)
8111 Melrose Avenue, Los Angeles, CA 90019 ☎ 323/653-3455

(Westbourne Dr.) **Men's and women's fashions** ▣ 🕐 *Mon.–Sat. 10am–6pm*

If you dream of looking like you stepped off the cover of a magazine, head to the flagship store of this exclusive label by Jonathan Meizler and German Valdivia. Discriminating fabrics, impeccable stitching and classic cuts are just some of the hallmarks of the Valdi style, which enjoys a sizeable celebrity following.

Off the Wall (42)
7325 Melrose Avenue, Los Angeles, CA 90046 ☎ 323/930-1185

(Fuller Ave) **Antiques, curios** ▣ 🕐 *Mon.–Sat. 11am–8pm*

Browsing at Off the Wall is like time-traveling through nearly a century of American pop culture. Their ever-changing assortment of kitsch and memorabilia might include giant jukeboxes, vintage neon signs, faux marble Greek statues or Depression-era radios. It's all arranged in a funky, haphazard fashion that never fails to amaze.

Necromance (43)
7220 Melrose Avenue, Los Angeles, CA 90046 ☎ 323/934-8684

(Alta Vista Blvd) **Curios** ▣ 🕐 *Mon.–Sat. noon–7pm; Sun. 1pm–7pm*

Gothic may no longer be the hot fad, but this store hasn't gone out of fashion. Seems like skulls and bones from animals and humans, mounted butterflies and insects, mice pickled in formaldehyde and positively spooky medical instruments do have a timeless appeal – to some. Come here for a slice of bizarre L.A. or even to indulge your own morbid fantasies.

Not forgetting

■ **Sacks SFO (44)** 652 N. La Brea, Los Angeles, CA 90036 ☎ 323/939-3993 *Low on decor but high on bargain fashions, Sacks SFO is a choice destination for L.A. hipsters on a budget. Update your own wardrobe – business suits to slinky gowns – with clothes by local and international designers, then get creative with their good selection of accessories. Check the Yellow Pages for another handful of branches around the city.*
■ **Wound & Wound Toy Shop (45)** 7374 Melrose Avenue, Los Angeles, CA 90046 ☎ 323/653-6703 *A selection of mechanical toys and musical boxes to make your head spin. There are things for all tastes and budgets, and even for collectors.*

Not quite as cutting-edge as it used to be, Melrose Avenue still ranks high among L.A.'s jazziest and fun shopping miles. Come here to soak up that L.A. vibe and shop for eccentric designs, cool clubwear, weird gifts and quirky accessories.

➡ # Where to shop

Curve (46)
154 N. Robertson Boulevard, Los Angeles, CA 90035 ☎ 310/360-8008

(Beverly Blvd) *Women's fashions* ▯ 🕐 *Mon.–Sat. 11am–7pm; Sun. noon–6pm*

For a peek at what celebrities like Mira Sorvino, Cameron Diaz and Jennifer Love-Hewitt will be wearing this season, visit this minimalist boutique that specializes in cutting-edge fashions from emerging designers, many of them Los Angeles-based. Also look for co-owner Delia Seaman's own line of clothing, plus jewelry designed by her partner, Nevena Borissova.

Storyopolis (47)
116 N. Robertson Boulevard, Los Angeles, CA 90035 ☎ 310/358-2500

(Alden Dr.) *Bookshop* ▯ 🕐 *Mon.–Sat. 10am–6pm; Sun. 10am–4pm*

This charming bookstore is stocked to the rafters with intelligent children's books from classic fairytales to Harry Potter to illustrated Bibles. The store displays limited edition prints of children's book illustrations and hosts readings and storytelling gatherings.

Harari (48)
110 N. Robertson Boulevard, Los Angeles, CA 90035 ☎ 310/275-3211

(Alden Dr.) *Women's fashions* ▯ 🕐 *Mon.–Sat. 10am–7.30pm; Sun. noon–6pm*

This beautiful, loft-type store – with a glass atrium and a real palm tree – is home to a striking collection of clothing. Whether you're looking for comfortable daytime wear or are in search of that slinky evening dress, you'll find it here. Silks, velvets and hand-printed fabrics with Chinese and Japanese patterns are the signature materials of this L.A.-based designer.

Village Studio (49)
130 S. Robertson Boulevard, Los Angeles, CA 90035 ☎ 310/274-3400

(3rd St.) *Articles for the home, jewelry, accessories* ▯ 🕐 *Mon.–Sat. 11am–6pm; Sun. noon–5pm*

Village Studio is really three stores in one. For some people, the main draw is the chic and flattering silver jewelry designed by Laura M, who counts Brooke Shields and Michelle Pfeiffer among her fans. There are paintings by California artists as well as unique ceramics, glassware, candlesticks and other gift items.

Not forgetting

■ **Loehman's (50)** 333 S. La Cienega Blvd, Beverly Hills, CA 90211 ☎ 310/659-0674 *Discounted mainstream designer clothing for the style-conscious man and woman with limited spending power.* ■ **New Stone Age (51)** 8407 W. Third St., Los Angeles, CA 90046 ☎ 323/658-5969 *Arts, crafts and knick-knacks from local and California artists, often with a whimsical, colorful touch.* ■ **Seaver (52)** 8360 W. Third St., Los Angeles, CA 90046 ☎ 323/653-8286 *Affordable and easy-to-wear styles from the Los Angeles designer Nathalie Seaver. A timeless look enlivened by highly contemporary touches.* ■ **Cook's Library (53)** 8373 W. Third St., Los Angeles, CA 90046 ☎ 323/655-3141 *Want to graduate from scrambling a couple of eggs? Check in here for possibly the world's largest assortment of cookbooks.*

The streets next to the Beverly Center mall are lined with elegant restaurants, cafes and designer boutiques. This district, with its hybrid and intense atmosphere, combines the creativity of West Hollywood ➡ 136 to the north with the sophistication of Beverly Hills ➡ 142 to the west.

In the area
◗ **Where to stay:** ➡ 24
◗ **Where to eat:** ➡ 50 ➡ 52 ➡ 56
◗ **After dark:** ➡ 70 ➡ 72
◗ **What to see:** ➡ 86 ➡ 102

Where to shop

The Cheese Store (54)
419 N. Beverly Drive, Beverly Hills, CA 90210 ☎ 310/278-2855

(Brighton Way) **Fine grocery** ▢ 🕐 *Mon.–Sat. 10am–6pm*

Cheese lovers will feel in heaven inside this exquisite store, a Beverly Hills institution since 1967. If the hundreds of hard-to-find cheeses, most of them imported from France, Italy, Switzerland and other countries, are confusing the friendly staff can make recommendations, even helping you choose the right wine to go along with your selection. Connoisseurs also stock up on foie gras, caviar and black and white truffles.

Williams-Sonoma (55)
339 N. Beverly Drive, Beverly Hills, CA 90210 ☎ 310/274-9127

(Brighton Way) **Articles for the home** ▢ 🕐 *Mon.–Sat. 10am–6pm; Sun. noon–5pm* ▢ *Beverly Center* ➡ 126

Whether you need a plastic spatula or a truffle grater, you'll find them here, along with top-quality pots and pans, small appliances and even beautifully packaged food products. There are also weekly in-store cooking classes and an oil and vinegar tasting bar. Various branches in L.A., including the Beverly Center ➡ 126.

Flora Design (56)
312 N. Beverly Drive, Beverly Hills, CA 90210 ☎ 310/274-9127

(Dayton Way) **Accessories** ▢ 🕐 *Mon.–Sat. 10am–7pm; Sun. noon–6pm*

This diminutive store looks a bit like a treasure trove out of an Arabian nights tale: here a basket spilling over with scrunchies, there a table smothered in colorful hair pins, next to a rack stacked with combs and a shelf brimming with hair bands; for a quick, inexpensive new look, ask about the Fun Bun, their signature creation.

The Wine Merchant (57)
9701 Santa Monica Blvd, Beverly Hills, CA 90210 ☎ 310/278-7322

(Roxbury Dr.) **Wines, spirits** ▢ 🕐 *Mon.–Fri. 9.30am–6pm; Sat. 10am–6pm* 🍷

When he opened this store in 1971, Dennis Overstreet knew exactly what his rich and famous clientele wanted: rare and delectable top-quality wines. His empire, vastly expanded since then, still gives priority to vintage wines, but they share the limelight with malts, caviar and cigars. You can taste over thirty wines in this elegant establishment, which turns into a bar after 4pm.

Not forgetting

◼ **Niketown (58)** 9560 Wilshire Blvd, Beverly Hills, CA 90212 ☎ 310/275-9998 *Like the New York store, this store delivers your goods to the till by a pneumatic system!* ◼ **Anthropologie (59)** 320 N. Beverly Dr., Beverly Hills, CA 90210 ☎ 310/385-7390 *Exotic layered clothing, gifts and accessories for the home in the flower-power mode. Branch on 1402 Third Street promenade, Santa Monica.* ◼ **A Gold E (60)** 9458 Brighton Way, Beverly Hills, CA 90210 ☎ 310/858-1844 *'For curious Americans' according to the publicity material. Very up-to-date jeans and sportswear for those who have graduated from Levi's and The Gap.*

Where to sho

Wild Oats Market (61)
500 Wilshire Avenue, Santa Monica, CA 90401 ☎ 310/395-8489

(5th St.) **Natural products** 🕐 *daily 8am–10pm* 🔢 *603 S. Lake Ave, Pasadena ☎ 626/792-1778; 8611 Santa Monica Blvd, West Hollywood ☎ 310/854-6927*

Organic tofu, meatless hamburgers, vegan pizza, lactose-free milk – health-food addicts will find everything they are looking for in this supermarket dedicated to their wellbeing and longevity. Take the opportunity to treat yourself to a relaxing session under the skillful fingers of the in-house masseur.

Banana Republic (62)
1202 Third St. Promenade, Santa Monica, CA 90401 ☎ 310/394-7740

(Wilshire Blvd) **Fashions** ▢ 🕐 *Mon.–Thu. 10am–9pm; Fri., Sat. 10am–11pm; Sun. 11am–10pm* 🔢 *357 N. Beverly Dr., Beverly Hills ☎ 310/858-7900*

A dramatic skylight sheds light over the extravagant Streamline Moderne entrance hall. Look for Banana Republic's wool, cotton, linen and leather clothing in a natural color palette, and also check out their new lines of jewelry, tableware, shoes and beauty products.

Restoration Hardware (63)
1221 Third St. Promenade, Santa Monica, CA 90401 ☎ 310/458-7992

(Wilshire Blvd) **Articles for the home** ▢ 🕐 *Mon.–Thu. 10am–9pm; Fri., Sat. 10am–10pm; Sun. 11am–8pm* 🔢 *Beverly Center, Pasadena ☎ 626/795-7234*

Sure, they've got doorknobs and gardening tools, but otherwise this isn't your run-of-the-mill hardware store. Walk through the various departments to find everything from a Violino auto sponge to a premium leather armchair, all beautifully presented. Furniture, gardenware, tools, household goods or bathroom fixtures, all are crafted, not just produced – and of high quality and in great taste.

Fred Segal (64)
500 Broadway, Santa Monica, CA 90401 ☎ 310/393-4477

(5th St.) **Fashions, accessories** ▢ 🕐 *Mon.–Sat. 10am–6pm; Sun. noon–6pm* 🔲

This cluster of boutiques is fashion nirvana for L.A. scenesters, as well as celebrities like Cameron Diaz and Helen Hunt. Racks of ultra-hip designer labels for men and women vie for attention with environmentally correct beauty products, hats, gift items, jewelry and hair accessories.

Not forgetting

■ **The Disney Store (65)** 1337 Third St. Promenade, Santa Monica, CA 90401 ☎ 310/576-6554 *Disney-themed products from key-chains to plates.*

■ **Puzzle Zoo (66)** 1413 Third St. Promenade, Santa Monica, CA 90401 ☎ 310/393-9201 *Possibly the world's largest puzzle collection, plus lots of games, clever and educational toys.*

■ **Hear Music (67)** 1429 Third St. Promenade, Santa Monica, CA 90401 ☎ 310/319-9527 *A treasure trove of ethnic and alternative music from all corners of the world, with helpful staff.*

Santa Monica is one of the best places to shop in LA. Most of the stores – from chains to one-of-a-kind boutiques – are concentrated along pedestrianized Third Street Promenade. Widen your choice by visiting Santa Monica Place ➡ 126.

66

63

STOP

ALL WAY

Areas of L.A.

Downtown L.A. serves as a reference point to find your way about. The Angelinos often refer to the following areas that you should recognize:

Midtown *area between Downtown L.A. a[nd] Beverly Hills taking in Koreantown and the Museum Mile on Mid-Wilshire*

Westside *Bel-Air, Brentwood, Westwood [and] Pacific Palisades*

South Bay *beach resorts including Venice, Manhattan Beach, Palos Verdes and Long*

San Gabriel Valley *(northeast) Pasadena, S[an] Marino, San Gabriel, Alhambra and Arcadia*

San Fernando Valley *comprises, among other places, Glendale and Burbank*

Los Angeles

The largest city in California and the second largest in the United States after Chicago. Los Angeles County spreads over more than 21,500 square miles and encompasses 88 towns with a total population of 14.5 million inhabitants.

6 Maps

Freeways

Names and numbers of the main freeways from Downtown

I-5 Golden State Fwy (northwest toward Baskerfield)
I-5 Santa Ana Fwy (southeast toward Irvine)
I-10 San Bernardino Fwy (east toward San Bernardino)
I-10 Santa Monica Fwy (west toward Santa Monica)
I-110 Harbor Fwy (south toward San Pedro)

I-110 Pasadena Fwy (north toward Pasadena)
I-210 Foothill Fwy (east)
I-405 San Diego Fwy (southeast)
I-605 San Gabriel River Fwy (south)
I-710 Long Beach Fwy (south)
US 101 Hollywood Fwy (northwest towards I-170)
US 101 Ventura Fwy (from I-134 north toward Ventura)

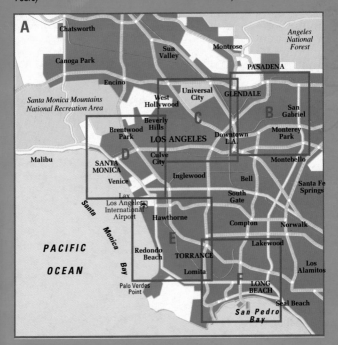

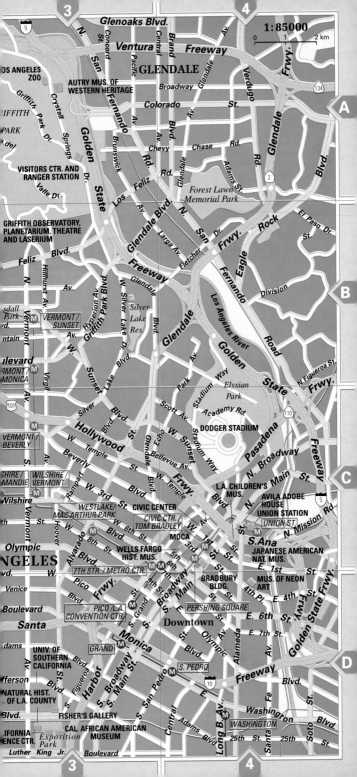

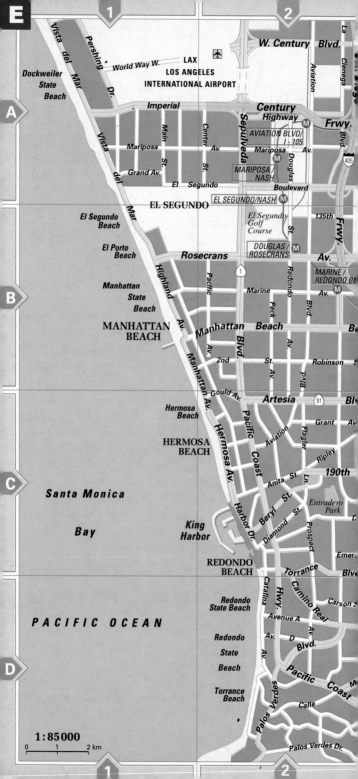

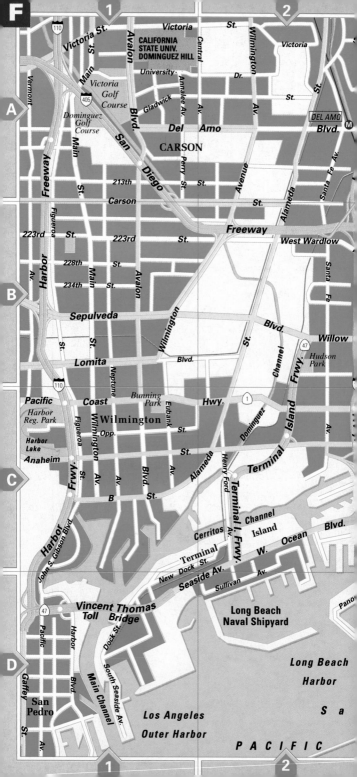

For each street, the letter in bold refers to one of the maps **(A–F)**, and the letters and numbers mark the corresponding square in which it is found.

Street
index

For practical and other information, as well as useful contact numbers concerning travel and life in Los Angeles, see the 'Getting there' section on pages 6 to 13.

General
index

Thanks to Nik Wheeler, to the Los Angeles and Long Beach Convention and Visitors Bureaux, and to all the establishments presented in this guide for their cooperation.

Picture
credits

Thanks to Nik Wheeler, to the Los Angeles and Long Beach Convention and Visitors Bureaux, and to all the establishments presented in this guide for their cooperation.

Picture
credits

I and cover illustration Denis Brumeaud
6 Gallimard / Sophie Lenormand
8-9 Gallimard / Sophie Lenormand, The Encounter - CA One Services, Inc / Tom Paiva
10-11 Gallimard / Sophie Lenormand
12-13 Gallimard / Patrick Léger (coins/ notes, newspapers, magazines), Gall. / S. Lenormand (telephone, Santa Monica Visitor Center, newspaper vending machines)
14 Casa del Mar
17 I Westin Bonaventure Hotel & Suites, 6 New Otani Hotel
19 8 Saga Motel, 9 Ritz Carlton Huntington Hotel & Spa, 10 Bissel B & B
21 17 Hollywood Roosevelt Hotel, 18 Highland Gardens Hotel
23 19 Gall. / Sophie Lenormand, 20 The Standard / Tod Eberly, 21 Mondrian Hotel, 22 Sunset Marquis Hotel & Villas, 24 Le Parc Suite Hotel
25 29 Regent Beverly Wilshire, 34 Four Seasons Beverly Hills
27 37 Bel-Air Hotel, 39 W
29 43 Channel Rd Inn, 44 Hotel Oceana, 46 Shangri-La, 51 Hotel Carmel
31 53 Hotel Casa del Mar, 54 Cadillac Hotel, 55 Gall. / S. Lenormand, 57 Shutters on the Beach, Gall. / Sophie Lenormand (vue extérieure)
33 61 Seaview Inn, 62 Gall. / S. Lenormand, 63 Portofino Hotel & Yacht Club
35 65 Lord Mayor's Inn, 66 Inn of Long Beach, 68 The Queen Mary

36 Nik Wheeler
39 I Ciudad, 2 Cafe Pinot / Grey Crawford, 3 Water Grill
41 Gall. / Sophie Lenormand (Chinatown), 8 Gall. / S. Lenormand, 9 Philippe the Original
43 11 Nik Wheeler, 13 Bistrot 45, 14 Parkway Grill
45 18 Gall. / Sophie Lenormand, 20 Patina, 21 Gall. / S. Lenormand
47 24 Gall. / Sophie Lenormand, 26 The Lobster
49 28 Jozu, 29 Lucques / Edmund Barr, 30 Nik Wheeler
51 36 Nate 'n' Al, 37 Crustacean, 38 Spago Beverly Hills, 39 Gall. / S. Lenormand
53 42 Gall. / Sophie Lenormand, 43 Campanile / Barry Michlin, 45 Nik Wheeler
55 46 La Cachette, 47 Woodside / Martin Cohen, 49 Bombay
57 53 Gall. / Sophie Lenormand, 54 Houston's, 55 Nik Wheeler
59 57 Nik Wheeler, 58 Nik Wheeler, 59 Il Fornaio, 61 El Cholo / Brian Leatart
61 63 Nik Wheeler, 67 C & O Trattoria / Larry A. Falke
63 70 Kincaid's, Gall. / S. Lenormand (vue extérieure)
65 75 L'Opéra, 77 Belmont Brewing, 78 The Queen Mary
66 Harvelle's
69 I North / Kelly Sedei, 4 Circle Bar
71 9 Yamashiro, 15 Three Clubs / Kelly Sedei
73 19 House of Blues, 22 Sky Bar
75 25 Nik Wheeler, 26 Silent Movie, 28 Nik Wheeler, 30 Nik Wheeler,

33 Ahmanson Theater / Craig Schwartz
77 36 Luna Park, Luna Park / Elena Dorfman (vues intérieures), 40 Gall. / S. Lenormand
79 43 Vynil, 47 The Derby
81 49 Catalina Bar & Grill, 50 Harvelle's, 51 Babe & Ricky's Inn
83 57 Garden of Eden, 59 The Playroom, 62 The Gate / Paul Dennler
84 Nik Wheeler
89 I Nik Wheeler, 6 Nik Wheeler, 7 L.A. Children Museum / Andrew Comins, 9 Nik Wheeler
91 10 The Natural History Museum of L.A. County, 13 Fisher's Gallery
93 14 The Gamble House / 1992 Thimothy Street-Porter, 16 Norton Simon Museum, 17 Nik Wheeler
95 21 Gallimard / Sophie Lenormand, 23 Autry Museum of Western Heritage / Susan Einstein, 24 Griffith Observatory / E.C. Kropp, 25 Gall. / S. Lenormand, 26 Nik Wheeler
97 27 Universal studios / 1999 Universal Studios (filming scene, King Kong, Return to the Future), Inc., Nik Wheeler (Prehistoric Tour), Gall./Sophie Lenormand (Universal logo), 29 Paramount Studios / LACVB - Michele & Tom Grimm
99 32 Gallimard / Sophie Lenormand, 35 Gall. / S. Lenormand, 36 Gall. / S. Lenormand, 37 Gall. / S. Lenormand
101 40 Gall. / Sophie Lenormand, 41 Los Angeles County Museum of Art, 42 Peterson Automotive Museum, 43 Carole & Barry Kaye Museum of Miniatures
103 45 City of Beverly Hills, 47 Museum of Television and Radio / Grant Mudford, 48 Museum of Tolerance
105 50 Nik Wheeler, 55 Nik Wheeler
107 56 LACVB / Michele & Tom Grimm, 59 LACVB / Michele & Tom Grimm, Gall. / S. Lenormand (Venice canals)

109 64 Nik Wheeler, 65 Nik Wheeler, 66 Gall. / S. Lenormand, 67 Nik Wheeler
111 69 Long Beach Aquarium of the Pacific / LACVB - Michele & Tom Grimm, 70 The Queen Mary / LACVB, 73 Gall. / Sophie Lenormand
112 Nik Wheeler
117 I Six Flags Magic Mountains / LACVB, 2 Nik Wheeler, 3 Nik Wheeler
119 7 Nik Wheeler, 8 Nik Wheeler, 9 Nik Wheeler, 11 Gall. / S. Lenormand, 13 Nik Wheeler
121 16 Nik Wheeler, 17 Nik Wheeler, 19 Nik Wheeler, 20 Nik Wheeler
123 22 Nik Wheeler, 23 Nik Wheeler
124 Gall. / Sophie Lenormand
126-127 I Gall. / Sophie Lenormand, 3 Century City Center
129 7 San Antonio Winery, 8 Nik Wheeler, 9 Gall. / Patrick Léger, 10 Gall. / S. Lenormand
131 14 Canyon Beachwear, 16 Distant Lands, 17 CP Shades, 19 Urban Outfitters / Vittoria Visuals
133 21 Hollywood Toys & Costumes, 24 Heaven 27, 25 Gall. / S. Lenormand
135 26 It's a Wrap, 27 Larry Edmunds, 31 Reel Clothes & Props
137 33 Gallimard / Sophie Lenormand, 34 Bodhi Tree, 35 Elixir Tonics & Teas, 36 Soolip Paperie & Soolip Bungalow
139 40 Jet Rag, 41 Jon Valdi, 43 Necromance, 45 Gall. / S. Lenormand
141 47 Storyopolis, 48 Harari, 49 Village Studio, 52 Seaver
143 54 The Cheesestore, 56 Flora Design, 58 Niketown L.A., 60 A Gold E
145 63 Restoration Hardware, 66 Gall. / S. Lenormand
146 Gallimard / Sophie Lenormand

168